Supporting EMI Students Outside of the Classroom

There is a growing body of research on English-medium Instruction (EMI) in Asian contexts, and much of this research points out difficulties experienced by stakeholders. This volume takes up the issue of support for EMI, which is, and which can be, offered to students outside of the classroom in order to help them succeed academically in an EMI environment. Dr Ruegg's book demonstrates the effectiveness of such support in the Japanese context. It begins by examining the support currently available for students in English-medium full degree programmes then goes on to examine one successful support service in more detail to determine the kinds of effects that can be achieved by establishing such a centre. The research reported in this book was conducted in Japan, but the findings will apply in other locations, especially in other Asian countries. The information provided in the book is expected to inform institutions who are looking to either establish an English-medium degree programme or improve on an existing programme by sharing information about the practices of other institutions.

Rachael Ruegg is a Senior Lecturer in the School of Linguistics and Applied Language Studies at Victoria University of Wellington, New Zealand.

Routledge Focus on English-Medium Instruction in Higher Education

The series pulls together experts from around the world who are at the cutting edge of research on EMI within higher education. It presents a balance of research-oriented voices and evidence-based practical guidance for EMI implementation. Contributions will address the phenomenon of EMI from a range of international contexts.

As EMI research and practice is growing quickly, the Routledge Focus short-form format is the ideal platform for this series. The books in the series will focus on contemporary developments in the field, providing concise, up-to-the-minute perspectives and examples to those involved in EMI planning and implementation.

Series Editors: Annette Bradford and Howard Brown

Professional Development for EMI Faculty in Mexico
The case of Bilingual, International, and Sustainable Universities
Myrna Escalona Sibaja

The Secret Life of English-Medium Instruction in Higher Education
Examining Microphenomena in Context
Edited by David Block and Sarah Khan

Student Motivation in English-Medium Instruction
Empirical Studies in a Japanese University
Naoko Kojima

Supporting EMI Students Outside of the Classroom
Evidence from Japan
Rachael Ruegg

To access the full list of titles, please visit: www.routledge.com/Routledge-Focus-on-English-Medium-Instruction-in-Higher-Education/book-series/RFEHE

Supporting EMI Students Outside of the Classroom
Evidence from Japan

Rachael Ruegg

LONDON AND NEW YORK

First published 2021
by Routledge
2 Park Square, Milton Park, Abingdon, Oxon OX14 4RN
and by Routledge
605 Third Avenue, New York, NY 10158

Routledge is an imprint of the Taylor & Francis Group, an informa business

© 2021 Rachael Ruegg

The right of Rachael Ruegg to be identified as author of this work has been asserted by her in accordance with sections 77 and 78 of the Copyright, Designs and Patents Act 1988.

All rights reserved. No part of this book may be reprinted or reproduced or utilised in any form or by any electronic, mechanical, or other means, now known or hereafter invented, including photocopying and recording, or in any information storage or retrieval system, without permission in writing from the publishers.

Trademark notice: Product or corporate names may be trademarks or registered trademarks, and are used only for identification and explanation without intent to infringe.

British Library Cataloguing-in-Publication Data
A catalogue record for this book is available from the British Library

Library of Congress Cataloging-in-Publication Data
A catalog record has been requested for this book

ISBN: 978-0-367-56396-7 (hbk)
ISBN: 978-0-367-56397-4 (pbk)
ISBN: 978-1-003-09752-5 (ebk)

Typeset in Times New Roman
by MPS Limited, Dehradun

Contents

List of figures vii
List of tables viii
Acknowledgements ix

1 **Introduction: English-medium instruction in the Japanese context** 1
   Background 1
   EMI implementation: Ideals 3
   EMI implementation: Realities 5
   EMI implementation: Challenges 8
   Suggestions for further growth 19
   References 20

2 **Initiatives for student support in full-degree EMI programmes in Japan** 24
   Background 24
   Incentives for offering student support 25
   Research on student support outside of Japan 26
   Student support in the Japanese context 28
   Support offerings in ETPs in Japan 30
   The current situation in ETPs in Japan 41
   References 45

3 **Case-study research investigating a support centre for EMI in Japan** 47
   Background 47
   Need for support services 49

Uptake of support 52
Peer support 53
Evaluation of support services 56
Linguistic background of tutors 58
The Academic Support Centre 60
Some centre history 63
Data and analysis 64
Usage of the centre 66
Student satisfaction 66
Qualitative reports of learning 68
Satisfaction and reported learning by linguistic background 76
Description of learning 77
Description of what went well or not so well 78
Discussion 81
References 88

4 Guidelines for supporting EMI students outside of the classroom 91
Getting started 91
Day to day operations 100
Enhancement 106
Bibliography 108

5 Conclusion: Supporting EMI students 110
Implications 113
Ongoing challenges 116
References 119

Appendix A: Survey on student support for English-medium instruction 120
Appendix B: Tutors' feedback questionnaire 123
Appendix C: Tutees' feedback questionnaire 124
Index 125

Figures

2.1	Age of EMI programmes	32
2.2	Dominant purpose of EMI instruction	33
2.3	Percentage of Japanese domestic students	34
2.4	Relationship between age of programme and support offered	35
2.5	Types of support offered	35
2.6	Who can receive support?	37
2.7	Who provides the support?	38
2.8	How often can students receive support?	40
2.9	Length of each support session	40

Tables

3.1	Reported learning of tutors	67
3.2	Satisfaction of tutors	67
3.3	Satisfaction of tutees	67
3.4	Reported learning of tutees	68
3.5	Satisfaction of tutees by tutor linguistic background	76
3.6	Reported learning of tutees by tutor linguistic background	76

Acknowledgements

I wish to express my sincere gratitude for the help and support of my former colleague, Dr Malcolm Sim. He is a dedicated and professional educator, and this book would not have been possible without his support and encouragement.

I would also like to acknowledge all the peer tutors I worked with during my time in Tohoku. It was a privilege to work with such an amazing group of young scholars, who had such enthusiasm and drive. As I've said so many times before, my door is always open for you.

1 Introduction: English-medium instruction in the Japanese context

Background

Increasing numbers of higher education institutions in Japan have started offering English-medium instruction. More specifically, a number of universities in Japan offer English-medium full-degree undergraduate programmes (English Taught Programmes, hereafter ETPs), and this number is continuing to increase. However, the implementation of undergraduate ETPs in Japan is not without challenges, and the challenges are not only faced by students but also by instructors. In addition to challenges for students and instructors, English-medium degree programmes may pose non-educational challenges.

Despite the significant challenges involved, this book takes the view that there is a great deal to be gained from the implementation of ETPs in Japan. However, if English-medium instruction (EMI) is to be implemented successfully, there are certain factors that need to be taken into consideration on the part of both the implementers and participants. While some institutions have had more success than others in implementing EMI in the Japanese context, there remains ample room for further development. The purpose of this volume is to better understand the support that is currently offered in undergraduate ETPs in Japan and to report on initiatives which have been trialled or implemented within EMI programmes in Japan and their success.

In the last few decades, there has been a change in the role of English in many educational institutions in countries where it is not the dominant language used in day-to-day communication: The introduction and rapid growth of English as a medium of instruction. English-medium instruction is defined by Dearden (2014, p. 4) as "The use of the English language to teach academic subjects in countries or jurisdictions where the first language (L1) of the majority of the population is not English." There are two points in this definition that are salient. Firstly, the focus of EMI study is on learning the subject matter at hand, not learning the language. As Wilkinson (2013) points out, not all students increase their English proficiency during EMI study, although they might become more adept or fluent in using the language they already know. Secondly, even if English is used as the medium of instruction, if it is also used for day-to-day communication in the same geographical region, then this would not be considered to fall under the umbrella of EMI. This is illustrated by the fact that Wächter and Maiworm (2015) excluded the United Kingdom, Ireland and Malta from their study of EMI in Europe, due to English being the dominant language in these countries.

Introducing EMI increases the role of English in the institution enormously. In non-Anglophone contexts, the majority of students are usually English as a Second Language (ESL) students. Therefore, firstly ESL students who study content classes in English will need to have reached a proficient level in their English language use. This introduces the need for more study of English as a language at earlier stages in their education, in order to prepare students for EMI classes. This can mean that EMI has a washback effect, encouraging primary and secondary schools to increase their English language education offerings. Alternatively, it can mean time is needed between secondary and tertiary study, in some kind of English for Academic Purposes (EAP) programme designed specifically to prepare students for tertiary study in the medium of English.

As well as language preparation for students who will participate in EMI education, institutions that offer EMI degree programmes need to ensure that there are faculty who are proficient in English and willing to teach in English and that there are resources available for English-medium study (such as books in the library). Since EMI by definition occurs in non-Anglophone countries, institutions that have previously been administered solely in the local language will need to set up English language versions of administrative procedures to cater to international students who become able to study at the institution by virtue of the implementation of EMI. Thus, what might appear on the surface as a simple change of instructional language has large implications which will be felt institutionwide. Essentially, the entire institution needs to reposition itself.

EMI was introduced mainly in the European context at first. This may have resulted from the role of English as a lingua-franca in this context. Wächter and Maiworm (2015) report that as of 2002, there were 725 EMI programmes in the 1558 higher education institutions they studied. They claim that in 2002, EMI was a "marginal phenomenon" in

Europe. However, they go on to report that the implementation of EMI programmes has increased from one programme per 2.15 higher education institutions in 2002 to a whopping 2.63 *programmes* per higher education *institution*, an increase of over 500% in a period of 12 years. However, it is by no means only in Europe that EMI has increased so rapidly. In fact, EMI has exploded around the world in such a way that Phillipson (2009) has labelled the trend a "pandemic" of teaching in English.

EMI implementation: Ideals

Attracting international students

English is the most widely spoken language around the world. There are such a large number of English speakers that offering education through the medium of English opens the doors of an institution to many more students than would otherwise be able to study there. As early as 1983, the Japanese Ministry of Education, Sport, Science and Technology (MEXT) introduced an internationalisation policy with the aim of increasing the number of incoming international students to 100,000 by the turn of the century (Takagi, 2009). When they reached the target, in 2003 (Hennings & Mintz, 2015), there were also around 75,000 Japanese students studying abroad (MEXT, 2015), creating a ratio of 1.3 incoming international students for every outgoing student. In 2008, the Japanese government took this aim higher and introduced the Global 30 Project, which aimed to double the number of incoming international students from 140,000 in 2008 to 300,000 by 2020. In addition, the project aimed to increase the diversity of international students, attracting more students from outside of East Asia. The basic idea of the Global 30 project was to increase the number of ETPs in Japan, facilitating an increased number of international students from a wider range of countries.

Fostering global competence in domestic students

In a context such as Japan, where English is not used as a lingua franca, instruction in the medium of English can also benefit domestic students, allowing increased opportunities to communicate in English and for experiences in intercultural communication. As early as 1997, a Japanese governmental report promoted the implementation of EMI programmes and stated that "it is also important for Japanese students, in addition to international students, to participate in these programs." (as cited in Tsuneyoshi, 2005, p. 67) One main benefit of Japanese student participation in such programmes is the development of global competence, which Morais and Ogden (2011) define as including awareness of oneself and one's own culture, intercultural communication skills and knowledge of global issues and events.

In 2012, the Global Human Resource Development project was introduced, which aimed "to overcome the Japanese younger generation's 'inward tendency' and to foster human resources who can positively meet the challenges and succeed in the global field, as the basis for improving Japan's global competitiveness and enhancing the ties between nations" (MEXT, n.d.a). In the Global Human Resource Development project, we see a primary focus on developing the skills of Japanese domestic students for the first time within MEXT policies related to the internationalisation of higher education. Research conducted by Bradford (2016a) found that the advantages of EMI for domestic students are often the main motivation for faculty to get involved in EMI programmes. She also states that, although in theory, EMI programmes may have been introduced to increase international students since international student numbers are so low many faculty in EMI programmes naturally focus more on the domestic student majority.

Literature relating to EMI demonstrates different benefits of EMI which are relevant to the development of global competence in domestic students. Taguchi (2005, p. 89) explains one benefit to Japanese students when they study in an EMI programme, "attainment of English skills is a by-product of the process of gaining content knowledge in academic subjects". In addition to content knowledge and language skills, EMI can also result in domestic students gaining an international outlook (de Jong & Teekens, 2003), developing intercultural skills (Van der Wende, 2000) and "new ideas and ways of thinking [can be] formed as a result of engagement with culturally different others" (Leask, 2009).

Improving the quality of education

Another motivation for the introduction of EMI is in an attempt to improve the quality of education. In the Japanese context, this occurs on two different levels: the Japanese government has encouraged the introduction of EMI in part to increase the overall quality of the Japanese higher education system. Evidence of this intention can be seen in the Top Global University Project (MEXT, n.d.b), which "through carrying out comprehensive reform and internationalization ... aims to enhance the international compatibility and competitiveness of higher education in Japan". At the same time, individual institutions have introduced

EMI departments or programmes to better compete with other domestic universities that also offer EMI programmes (Brown, 2014). Kitahama (2003) states that increasing the educational quality of universities is the most crucial factor in increasing the number of international students. Similarly, Wilkinson (2013) states that it is not the language of instruction which motivates a student to join a particular department or university but the perceived quality of the education on offer in that department or university.

One aspect of increasing the quality of education may be offering a wider range of perspectives on content matter, in order for students to gain deeper and more nuanced understanding. Another aspect of increasing educational quality may be incorporating a wider range of teaching and learning practices. Both of these can be achieved through the recruitment of a greater number of international faculty, who are likely to bring with them a wider range of past educational experiences and a more diverse range of perspectives on content matter (Lassegard, 2006). International faculty not only bring different teaching and learning styles and offer students a wider range of perspectives on their content area, but they can also be a source of alternative methods and ideas for local faculty (Chapple, 2014). By incorporating a wider range of teaching and learning styles, universities will succeed in getting through to a wider range of both international and domestic students. Moreover, by introducing students to a wider range of perspectives, universities will be more successful in fostering globally-minded students, both international and domestic.

EMI implementation: Realities

Dominance of English

The dominance of English on the global level is the main reason for introducing EMI in most places, including Japan, and the field of education is no exception in terms of the dominance of English. The last time universities shared a common language, universities were institutions for the elite, and the language was Latin (Nastansky, 2004). Currently, this appears to be happening again, but the language is English. Most significantly, universities are no longer the reserve of the elite. Thus, the dominance of one language at universities is more likely to spell the dominance of the language in general. There are many indicators of the growing dominance of English as the language of higher education. Faculty in higher education institutions are encouraged to publish, and even those who do not publish research themselves draw on the research of others for their class content. Estimates of the proportion of academic publications published in English range from 74% to 95% (Bidlake, 2008). Similarly, Ammon (2012) found that 76% of publications in the social sciences and over 90% in the natural sciences were published in English by 2005. Furthermore, many are encouraged to publish in "international peer-reviewed journals". In practice, publishing in an "international peer-reviewed journal" may be almost equal to publishing in English. Tardy (2004, p. 249) states that this "lead[s] to a self-perpetuating cycle in which English becomes increasingly important".

Along with the increase in the importance of English for university teaching staff, the numbers of international students have also been rapidly increasing. According to Wächter and Maiworm (2008), there were 600,000 international tertiary students in 1975, and this had increased to 2,700,000 by 2005, an increase of 450% in a period of 30 years. As the number of international students increased, English-speaking countries had a distinct advantage due to the wide use of English. Other countries started in introduce EMI programmes in order to have more strength in attracting international students. Indeed, according to the OECD (2016), the four countries with the highest ratio of incoming to outgoing international students were Australia, the United Kingdom, the United States and New Zealand. On average, these four countries receive 13.6 international students for every one they send abroad (OECD, 2016). They are also the only four countries with ratios which are more than double the OECD average of three incoming students for every one outgoing. It is perhaps not a coincidence that these represent four of the five inner-circle countries (Kachru, 1982) in which English has historically been the dominant language. Many students study abroad in Anglophone countries due to the advantage that English language proficiency can offer. The benefits of knowing English come about because English has established such a dominant position as a global lingua franca. Paradoxically, dominance begets dominance when it comes to languages. English has been described as a "near-essential tool of a flexible, mobile labour force" (Enever, 2009). Others have described a current or future diglossic world, in which the local language is used for day-to-day communication and English is used for formal communication (Coleman, 2006; Taguchi, 2005).

Domestic students

Although there are no objective indices of language proficiency levels of learners on a global scale, Japanese are often considered to have low English proficiency levels, compared to many other countries (e.g. Morita, 2015; Tsuneyoshi, 2005). An article in The Japan Times (2019) reported that the Japanese government's English language proficiency target was Eiken pre-2 level or above (the equivalent of CEFR level A2, a total score of 32 on TOEFL iBT, or 3.0 on IELTS). Some may consider the level to be quite unambitious after six years of compulsory English language study. Despite the unambitious target, the majority of students failed to meet it in 2018 (The Japan Times, 2019). Education First (2017), one of the few organisations which attempt to compare English language proficiency levels across countries, evaluates the average Japanese person's language proficiency level as "Low". Not only students, but even English teachers in Japan have failed to meet up to the Japanese government's expectations. According to an article in Nikkei Asian Review (2016), the Japanese government set Eiken pre-1 level (the equivalent of CEFR level C1, a total score of 79 on TOEFL iBT or 6.5 on IELTS) as the proficiency benchmark for Japanese teachers of English at the secondary school level. However, the article reports that only 30% of junior high school teachers and 57% of high school teachers had achieved the benchmark by the beginning of the 2016 academic year.

Before the explosion of EMI, English was usually used as a medium of instruction only during English language classes in most non-Anglophone contexts, that is, English was not chosen specifically as the medium for delivering the content matter, but rather the target language was used within the classroom in order for students to practice communicating in the language. However, the use of English as a medium of instruction even in the English as a foreign language classroom in primary and secondary schools in Japan has still not taken root. MEXT introduced a new course of study in 2009 which specified that teachers should, in principle, teach English in English from the beginning of the 2013 academic year. However, MEXT (2016a) data from 2015 shows the number of teachers who self-reported using mostly English when teaching English language classes at the secondary school level. The numbers of teachers responding this way in relation to different English language courses ranged from 34% to 50%, indicating that two years after the policy was implemented the majority of English language teachers were still teaching English mainly in Japanese.

EMI in Japan

MEXT (2011, as cited in Brown, 2018, p. 3) defines EMI classes as "classes which are conducted entirely in English, excluding those whose primary aim is language education." This also implies that not only do the classes themselves need to be conducted in English, but any required readings and assignments also need to be conducted in English. However, the EMI label has often been misused in Japan, with many educators and researchers in the Japanese context referring to English language classes which are taught in the target language as EMI classes and some using the term to refer to bilingual classes. This ambiguity in the meaning of the term in the Japanese context also causes difficulty when identifying the number of such courses offered in Japan. There are no completely accurate and up-to-date figures available for the number of EMI courses offered at universities in Japan. However, MEXT (2019) reports that as of 2016, 100 of the 777 universities in Japan were offering some form of English-medium instruction (16%). However, a majority of those universities appear to be offering EMI classes on an ad hoc basis. Being included in this count could potentially indicate that only one EMI class is offered university-wide. Brown (2018) also found that in most universities, EMI classes were taken by less than 10% of the students on campus. Thus, EMI appears to be a small and somewhat peripheral phenomenon, albeit widespread.

Due to the large number of universities offering EMI classes, the inconsistency in the use of the term and the consequent difficulty in identifying instances of true EMI, this book will focus on undergraduate ETPs. ETPs are programmes, departments, or universities from which a student can graduate after having only taken classes in English. Not only are these the kinds of programmes which typically attract non-Japanese speaking international students to Japan but they are also the kinds of programmes that the Japanese government encouraged through the introduction of the Global 30 project. ETPs are still relatively rare in Japan, although their numbers are increasing rapidly. Morizumi (2015) reported that there were only five universities offering full-degree ETPs in 2006 (Akita International University, International Christian University, Ritsumeikan Asia Pacific University, Sophia University and Waseda University). MEXT (2011) identified 27 individual ETPs within 16 universities in Japan. MEXT (2019) provided an updated list, which included 65 individual ETPs within 38 different universities. The identified undergraduate ETPs will be the focus of this book. This is not intended to suggest that the ideas in the book do not apply to ad hoc EMI classes that make up only a part of a student's undergraduate studies.

EMI implementation: Challenges

As stated above, higher education institutions need to prepare a great deal to implement EMI at all. The preparations include ensuring students are prepared, hiring or training faculty to teach in English and adapting administrative processes. These preparations are very closely linked to the challenges that are commonly faced in the Japanese context after the implementation of EMI.

Challenges for students

Firstly, and perhaps most importantly, there are many challenges for students who enter EMI programmes. Even in the current era of globalisation, the population in Japan is fairly homogenous. However, this is not the case within EMI programmes. Some of the greatest benefits of EMI programmes come from this multicultural environment, whereas this multicultural environment also causes many challenges. Most of the challenges come from the fact that the population within EMI programmes is not homogenous, and each different group of students has different expectations and needs.

The primary expectation of most students entering any higher education institution is to learn content matter in their field/s of study. The first challenge stems from the different educational backgrounds through which students have come, which mean that they have vastly different amounts of background knowledge. In each country, secondary schools have certain requirements, and the tertiary education sector of a country usually expects that all students who enter university meet those requirements. However, the requirements vary greatly between countries. For example, students in Japan are expected to have relatively shallow knowledge in a broad range of subject areas. On the other hand, the education system in England takes the opposite approach, secondary school students there specialise much earlier and are expected to develop a much deeper knowledge of as few as three subject areas by the end of secondary school. These differences cause various difficulties. In the Japanese context, there is a great deal of standardisation of the secondary school curriculum, so it can reasonably be expected that all university students will have a rudimentary knowledge of the French revolution, for example. An English student who has not taken history at the secondary school level may not have that knowledge although they are likely to have a deeper understanding of the subjects they did study than a student who completed secondary school in Japan.

A different kind of challenge arises from the different subjects even offered in different countries' secondary education sectors. Students who major in business in New Zealand would typically be expected to have taken business subjects throughout secondary school. For example, it would not be uncommon for a student to have taken "Business Studies" (a combined class on Economics and Accounting) at the year 9 and 10 levels and to have taken both Economics and Accounting at the year 11, 12 and 13 year levels. In this situation, they would have studied business-related subjects for four to five years at the secondary level. On the other hand, the secondary school curriculum in Japan rarely includes any accounting or economics, and students would be expected to enter university with no specific knowledge related to business subjects. These kinds of differences in education systems at the secondary school level cause difficulties for both teachers and students at the tertiary level. Faculty ultimately need to decide where to pitch the level of their course content and risk leaving some students behind and/or boring other students. In these ways, the multicultural environment can cause challenges for students, and it may require extra effort both inside and outside of the classroom to keep up with the class content and/or to supplement the classroom learning to maintain interest.

The second challenge related to the acquisition of content knowledge is large variations in language proficiency between students. A student who has a low level of English language proficiency may simply not be ready to acquire any content knowledge in an English-medium context. Thus, the implementation of EMI in Japan has introduced the need for preparatory language study either at the primary and/or secondary school level or in a pre-sessional EAP programme.

In a pre-sessional EAP programme, students can reach the requisite level of English language proficiency before progressing to content instruction in the medium of English. In theory, this sounds like a sound solution to the language proficiency problem. However, in practice, there are many complications that come about in the pre-sessional EAP model. Since students will be using the English language, they learn for academic purposes, English for Academic Purposes (EAP) should be taught. EAP differs from regular English language courses in its content and skills. The content used for the language instruction would typically be academic in nature; such as (simplified) texts taken from textbooks and academic lectures. The course would likely focus on skills such as listening to academic lectures, note-taking, research and writing academic essays. These are different from the kind of approach usually found in general English courses, which may focus on carrying out day-to-day interactions in English, having casual conversations and writing e-mails, for example. However, Brown (2016) found that only 8% of the EMI offering institutions in his study offered pre-sessional or concurrent EAP to students. He also mentioned that even when EAP is offered, it is often taught as a general education class or in preparation for study abroad rather than specifically focussed on preparing students for EMI study in the Japanese context. Brown (2018, p. 69) sees this as an indication that "some universities in Japan see ETPs rather simplistically and are underestimating the needs of students".

There are challenges for students related to the language proficiency tests that they take. IELTS could be seen as the most authentic test of academic English because the tasks are fairly authentic. Learners are required to pass multiple-choice style tests of receptive language comprehension proficiency (listening and reading), to take part in an interview with a live interviewer (a relatively authentic experience in oral communication) and to write two different styles of essay which are rated by human raters (a relatively authentic written communication task). However, the price for this relatively authentic assessment process is high, because human raters need to be employed, trained and paid. Another suitable test of academic English is the TOEFL iBT. The TOEFL iBT consists of similar multiple-choice style listening and reading sections and sections that assess speaking and writing skills. However, in order to offer the test more efficiently and cheaply, the interview section of the TOEFL iBT test takes place between the test taker and a computer. Talking to a computer could be considered a relatively inauthentic task. On the other hand, the writing tasks in TOEFL iBT involve reading and listening as well as writing and may be considered relatively authentic in the context of academic writing where it is common to read information and listen to lectures in order to prepare for writing an essay.

A less suitable test is the TOEFL ITP (Institutional Testing Programme), which contains no test of language production, only two multiple-choice sections of receptive (listening and reading) proficiency and a "written expression" section which tests a test-takers' explicit knowledge of English grammatical rules. Unfortunately, the TOEFL ITP is by far the cheapest test and is commonly used in Japan. If the TOEFL ITP is used as proof of English language proficiency for admission to an EMI programme, there is no way of knowing whether the student will be able to speak or write in English at even the most basic level, as only their receptive proficiency and explicit knowledge of grammatical rules have been tested. Apart from the TOEFL ITP, the TOEIC is also commonly used in the Japanese context as proof of English language proficiency for students who wish to enter EMI programmes. The TOEIC is not only a purely receptive test but a test of business English, rather than of academic English. Therefore, using it as a placement, progress or academic achievement test is arguably authentic in the context of a business English course, certainly not in an EAP context.

It has been reported (e.g. Brown, 2016; Toh, 2014) that in some universities in Japan which offer EMI classes, no language proficiency benchmarks are in place and any student can enrol for the classes. This means that they may lack not only productive English language proficiency but any English language proficiency at all. In fact, Brown (2016) found that 70% of the universities offering EMI classes in his study did not have language proficiency benchmarks in place. In another case, an academic shared the difficulties of conducting successful EMI in Japan, also reporting that students with TOEFL ITP scores as low as 470 (equivalent to CEFR level B1, a score of 4.0 on IELTS, or around 50 on TOEFL iBT) were taking the EMI classes in the context in question (Kojima, 2016). Similarly, in the context described by Toh (2014) some students entered the EMI programme at the false-beginner level, and after two semesters of study in the EMI programme, they still tested at the false-beginner level. If students with an English proficiency level as low as this are allowed to take content classes in the medium of English, then it is not surprising that many implementers of EMI in Japan have encountered enormous challenges along the way.

Even when second language learners have taken a suitable language proficiency test and achieved a suitable score, this does not guarantee that they have sufficient English language skills to succeed in the EMI context (Kelo & Rogers, 2010; Röemer, 2002). Most educators will have experienced students who do well on tests but perform poorly on classroom activities, just as there are some who are competent in classroom activities but perform poorly in tests.

Apart from learning content knowledge, a large number of non-native speakers of English enter an EMI programme with an expectation that learning content matter in English will automatically lead to incidental language proficiency improvement. Indeed, several previous studies have found that in some cases, this is the only reason for students to take English-medium courses (Galloway, Numajiri, & Rees, 2020; Ishikura, 2015). As mentioned already, not all students increase their English proficiency during EMI study, although they might become more adept or fluent in using the language they already know (Wilkinson, 2013).

The above example from Toh (2014) demonstrates that students are unlikely to achieve improved language proficiency unless they are already at a certain proficiency level, which allows them to understand class contents in English. Indeed, universities admitting students who have not reached a sufficient level of English proficiency to understand content classes in English introduces a great deal of cognitive pressure for students. Airey (2011) found that when non-native English-speaking students attended lectures in English, they were less likely to ask questions than when they attended lectures in their first language. Japanese students are already often reluctant to ask questions in class and attending classes in English may be one factor that decreases the number of questions they ask even further. Airey (2011) also found that it was difficult for students attending classes in their L2 to listen and take notes at the same time. They could listen and understand the content of the lecture, or they could take appropriate notes, but not simultaneously. Hellekjaer (2010) also documented non-native speakers of English having difficulties taking notes when attending English-medium lectures. Clearly, students who attend university lectures need to listen to (and understand) lectures and take appropriate notes. It appears that not only do students not automatically increase their language proficiency through attending English medium classes but that any language proficiency increases that do occur are well-earnt gains which come about only through considerable and sustained effort.

Despite the extra effort needed on the part of students, insufficient language proficiency can result in receiving lower grades for EMI courses. Some students at Japanese universities choose not to enrol in EMI programmes or not to take EMI courses because they do not want to damage their grade point average (GPA) (Bradford, 2016b). Similarly, those who do take EMI courses or programmes may forsake a higher GPA to do so.

Challenges for faculty

The multicultural and multilingual make-up of the student body by no means poses challenges only to students. It also poses a great many challenges to faculty who are charged with teaching courses in EMI programmes. It poses challenges regardless of the cultural and linguistic make-up of the faculty body. However, different aspects of the faculty body make-up result in different kinds of challenges.

When a programme markets itself as "international", as many EMI programmes in Japan do, students and parents may expect the faculty to also be international. Indeed, as mentioned above, internationalisation means more than simply offering the same class content that has always been taught but translating it into English. One important aspect of internationalisation is the incorporation of a range of international perspectives on content matter, fostering students with an international outlook. It appears that so far mainly Japanese faculty have been tasked with offering classes in EMI programmes in Japan. MEXT (2016b) data shows that as of 2015, only 4% of all full-time university staff in Japan were non-Japanese.

If faculty are employed to teach on EMI programmes whose first language is not English, then not only the language proficiency skills of students but even the language proficiency skills of faculty members may pose difficulties. Indeed, the language proficiency of faculty has been found to create more challenges than that of students (Kelo & Rogers, 2010). Wilkinson (2013) reports that students expect content teachers to be relatively proficient in English, although it is invariably their second language. Students often feel that this expectation has not been satisfied and express dissatisfaction with the English proficiency of content faculty (Ammon & McConnell, 2002; Galloway & Ruegg, 2020). Insufficient language proficiency creates challenges for faculty in the form of difficulty in communicating the content clearly, in elaborating and improvising during lectures (Wilkinson, 2013). Faculty have also reported that their lectures can become dry and technical because it is difficult to add anecdotes or use more casual language when lecturing in a second language (Wilkinson, 2005) These language difficulties may cause students to doubt faculty members' content knowledge (Vinke, 1995).

As a possible solution to the problem of deficiencies in faculty members' English language proficiency, Vinke (1995) suggested that not only students but also faculty members' language proficiency should be screened before they start teaching in an EMI programme. The English proficiency of faculty who will teach in EMI programmes may be seen as an important aspect to consider during employment decision-making. There is also a tendency for faculty with postgraduate qualifications gained abroad, usually in English speaking countries, to be prioritised in the Japanese context (e.g. Lassegard, 2006).

Even when a faculty member is proficient enough to conduct successful lectures in English, preparing and conducting lectures in a second language will invariably be more time consuming (Vinke, 1995). Tsuneyoshi (2005) suggested that teaching in English increased the time spent by Japanese faculty members by four to five times. Participants in Bradford's (2016b) study stated that teaching in an EMI programme in Japan did increase their workload, but not by as much as Tsuneyoshi (2005) suggested. Clearly, preparing for lectures in a second language does increase the amount of time needed for faculty to fulfil the same teaching load in their first language. However, the extent of this increase probably varies considerably between individuals and remains somewhat opaque.

The increased time and effort required to prepare and conduct lectures in English may suggest the lectures conducted in an EMI programme should be weighted more heavily in terms of the total workload a faculty member is required to carry out. Vinke (1995) suggested temporarily exempting faculty from administrative duties when they are offering classes in English for the first time. However, Tsuneyoshi (2005) found that quite the opposite was the case. EMI courses were not counted towards a faculty member's teaching load, instead being added as a "voluntary" time contribution. Moreover, this arrangement was found not only in one university but at a number of universities investigated. Ultimately, these kinds of administrative practices cause challenges for students more than faculty. This is because these kinds of policies and practices will inevitably manifest in a reduction in the quality and quantity of content that can be shared with students.

Each country has its own educational culture. As Coleman (2006, p. 10) puts it

> The distinctive approaches to lecturing in Italian, Spanish or German universities are currently part of the benefit of student exchanges, making young people question the narrowly ethnocentric, monocultural perspectives which too many of them take abroad, and a key element in developing their intercultural competence, their recognition that cultural norms are relative and not absolute, socially constructed and not given.

Programme implementers in Bradford's (2016b, p. 346) study believed that "it is possible to separate EMI from its dominant cultures and teach in English using a more traditional Japanese pedagogic approach". Employing too many international faculty may detract from the educational culture present in Japan, an educational culture which some international students may be specifically seeking when choosing to study in Japan.

On the other hand, the whole concept of "internationalization" would seem to necessitate cultural change within the education system. Even if Japanese faculty alone are employed to teach in the EMI programmes in Japan, it seems likely that offering programmes in the medium of English to a culturally mixed group of students will encourage, or even necessitate, this kind of cultural change, since students will be coming from vastly different backgrounds in terms of teaching style, expected classroom behaviour, assessment practices and faculty evaluation. Different faculty having different expectations and the expectations not being explicitly conveyed to students will likely lead to a lack of understanding on the part of the students of how to behave in each classroom (Lassegard, 2006).

Although the main purpose of the Global 30 Project was to increase the number of EMI programmes in Japan in order to increase the number of international students studying at Japanese universities, the number of international students is still relatively low. At the university level, and even at the classroom level, there are often not enough international students in the classroom to make English the most effective medium of instruction (Bradford, 2016b). At the most extreme end of the spectrum, a Japanese faculty member could be faced with an EMI class consisting of only Japanese students. In this case, it would seem that, since the students have registered for an EMI class and the faculty member is tasked with teaching an EMI class, the class should be conducted in English. However, this creates, at best an inauthentic context and at worst, a somewhat awkward situation. Not only does the lack of international students impose an inauthentic domain for English language use, it may ultimately result in a curriculum created with Japanese domestic students in mind, a curriculum that may not serve international students well when they are present.

Another aspect of faculty that may pose challenges when teaching in the EMI context is their disciplinary background. As outlined above, students expect to learn content knowledge as well as to improve their English proficiency level. However, it is unlikely for an individual faculty member to have expertise in both a content area and linguistics. In Brown's (2018) investigation of nine universities with ETPs, six of the universities stated that they employed content specialists or mainly content specialists, while three indicated that they employed a balance of content specialists and language specialists. It is unrealistic to expect a content area faculty member to be an expert in applied linguistics, just as it is unrealistic to employ an applied linguist to teach a content area other than applied linguistics or language. In an ideal world, faculty would be able to be found for EMI programmes that had a background in both applied linguistics and a content area, but this is a hard ask in the real world. Since these kinds of faculty are extremely hard to come by, it would be beneficial for content area specialists and applied linguists to work together to develop and apply the curriculum, to prepare and provide classes and to support students in their learning. However, 15% of universities in Costa and Coleman's (2013) study reported that the lack of such collaboration between language teachers and content area teachers was their greatest challenge. In the East Asian context, too, research has demonstrated a lack of collaboration between language and content instructors (Galloway, Numajiri & Rees, 2020).

It has been a tradition for quite some time for individuals with a doctorate in any subject to be deemed as qualified to teach that subject at the tertiary level. The fact that the individual may have no knowledge of education or teaching skills has been considered irrelevant. Perhaps someone who had so much experience on the receiving end of education would experience the incidental acquisition of teaching skills. In the current era of globalisation, especially in the EMI context, the wide range of students from different linguistic, educational and cultural backgrounds greatly increase the number of skills needed by teachers if they are to succeed in conveying the class content to all the students in their classrooms. Faculty who are tasked with educating students require effective communication skills and strong interpersonal skills. In addition to this, in the current era, and especially in the context of EMI, faculty also require a high degree of intercultural communication skills and knowledge of effective pedagogy. Many EMI researchers have stated that there are challenges that arise not from the language proficiency level of faculty, but rather from a perceived lack of cross-cultural awareness (Kelo & Rogers, 2010; Leask, 2009) or pedagogical awareness among faculty (Lassegard, 2006).

Non-educational challenges

What is apparent is that the internationalisation of education is a very challenging process. It is a process that involves a great deal of forethought, planning and cross-cultural understanding. There is often an assumption that it is international students who should travel the whole distance in terms of adapting to the host culture (Leask, 2009). However, intercultural interaction is a reciprocal relationship, which requires adaptations on both sides (Leask, 2009).

Both anecdotally and in literature on the topic, international students studying in Japan have complained of being socially excluded. Students in Bradford's (2016b) study, for example, expressed frustration at being regarded as short-term international students when they were actually international degree-seeking students who would spend four years at the university like their Japanese counterparts. This situation is further complicated by the confusing way in which the two groups are defined. Students are identified based on their citizenship rather than the ethnicity with which they identify, and other factors such as linguistic knowledge or cultural background often seem to play very little role. This approach to identification may have been appropriate until fairly recently due to the relatively homogenous composition of Japanese society. However, it can no longer be assumed that a person who is a Japanese citizen is a domestic student culturally or linguistically and increasingly the same can be said for non-Japanese citizens. This increasing diversity complicates such definitions. It also causes problems when it comes to offering support to students. Students with various different backgrounds require different kinds of support. Classifying students into simplistic categories may lead to misconceptions about issues such as cultural capital and language proficiency. Such confusion as to a student's background could ultimately lead to support not being available to those for whom it is necessary.

Even within the educational institutions in which they study, students might find that all administration is conducted entirely in Japanese, targeting the Japanese domestic student population. This can result in a situation whereby international students require excessive amounts of support with administrative procedures. Such extra support could be avoided by providing bilingual administrative processes. Students may also become socially isolated when they find that outside of the EMI classroom no English is spoken on campus and even computer laboratories may not be installed with English versions of programmes (Kelo & Rogers, 2010).

There are also various challenges for both international and domestic students' prospects after graduation. At most Japanese universities, no additional support is available for international students who seek to work in Japan after graduation (e.g. Breaden, 2013), which makes it difficult for international students to remain in Japan in any capacity other than as a language teacher. Moreover, throughout Japan university career and employment offices often fail to consider or cater to any students who choose to work overseas after graduation. This encourages Japanese domestic students who are internationally minded and globally competent to be at a loss as to how to find work internationally. In this case, many may give up their international dreams in favour of a position in Japan. Leask (2009, p. 208) states that in the era of globalisation being globally competent is an important skill because "all graduates will work in a global setting." If there is no assistance for international students to find employment in Japan after graduation and no assistance for Japanese domestic students to find employment outside of Japan, this assumes that international students will leave Japan upon graduation and Japanese students will stay.

Suggestions for further growth

"It seems clear that using English touches on very deep-seated cultural and social issues which far exceed simply changing the language of instruction" (Tsuneyoshi, 2005, p. 73). Some may feel that universities should desist from EMI and revert to English as a foreign language instruction given all the challenges mentioned above. However, there is a great deal to be gained from persisting with EMI.

If EMI is to be implemented successfully, there are certain factors that need to be taken into consideration on the part of the implementers and participants. Firstly, it is important that anyone entering an EMI course has sufficient English language proficiency to understand class contents in the English medium. Implementers of ETPs and programmes of study that include EMI courses could decrease the challenges involved in the implementation of EMI by setting reasonable English language proficiency benchmarks for entry. Students who are proficient enough in English to enter a university in an Anglophone country should also be proficient enough to study in an EMI programme in a non-Anglophone country. Therefore, a language proficiency benchmark of approximately 80 on the TOEFL iBT (550 on TOEFL ITP, 6.5 on IELTS or CEFR level C1) would be a good benchmark to reach before entering pure EMI content classes. In a sheltered programme in which students study the English language and take EMI classes at the same time, this could be a little lower. Putting English language proficiency benchmarks in place is probably the factor that will have the most profound effect on the success of an EMI programme.

Students should also consider how much English they are able to understand in an English immersion environment and reflect on how much pressure will be involved if they are unable to understand much. This should help them to make a sound decision regarding the suitability of EMI for them. Students should be advised to consider not only their language proficiency but also their motives in entering an EMI programme. EMI is a challenging road which should not be taken lightly.

Other important factors that implementers of EMI should take into consideration relate to the employment of suitable educational and administrative staff and systems. Institutions should carefully consider which faculty would be the most appropriate for each course of study and ensure that administrative staff can function in English. It would also save a great deal of future time and effort if all administrative systems and documents were available in English for programmes that are marketed to international students.

Some institutions have had more success than others in implementing EMI. Bradford (2013, p. 235) suggests that "going forward, Japanese universities will benefit from documenting their experiences with EMI, recording their lessons learned, and sharing best practices". That is exactly the purpose of this book. The book comprises studies carried out in EMI programmes in the Japanese context relating to supporting students outside of the classroom. The studies were conducted to better understand current support practices in EMI programmes in Japan, to better understand the challenges faced by faculty and students who are involved in ETPs in Japan and to report on support initiatives which have been trialled or implemented within EMI programmes and the relative success of those initiatives.

References

Airey, J. (2011). The relationship between teaching language and student learning in Swedish University physics. In B. Preisler, I. Klitgard, & A. H. Fabricius (Eds.). *Language and learning in the international university: From English uniformity to diversity and hybridity* (pp. 3–18). Multilingual Matters.

Ammon, U. & McConnell, G. (2002). *English as an academic language in Europe*. Peter Lang.

Ammon, U. (2012). Linguistic inequality and its effects on participation in scientific discourse and on global knowledge accumulation–With a closer look at the problems of the second-rank language communities. *Applied Linguistics Review, 3*(2), 333–355. https://doi.org/10.1515/applirev-2012-0016

Bidlake, E. (2008). Whose voice gets read? English as the International Language of Scientific Publication. *e-pisteme, 1*(1), 3–21.

Bradford, A. (2013). English-medium degree programs in Japanese universities: Learning from the European experience. *Asian Education and Development Studies, 2*(3), 225–240. https://doi.org/10.1108/AEDS-06-2012-0016

Bradford, A. (2016a). Teaching content through the medium of English: Faculty perspectives. In P. Clements, A. Krause, & H. Brown (Eds.). *Focus on the learner*. JALT.

Bradford, A. (2016b). Toward a typology of implementation challenges facing English-medium instruction in higher education: Evidence From Japan. *Journal of Studies in International Education, 20*(4), 339–356. https://doi.org/10.1177/1028315316647165

Breaden, J. (2013). *The organizational dynamics of university reform in Japan: International inside out*. Routledge.

Brown, H. G. (2014). Contextual factors driving the growth of undergraduate English-medium instruction programmes at universities in Japan. *The Asian Journal of Applied Linguistics, 1*(1), 50–63. https://caes.hku.hk/ajal/index.php/ajal/article/view/18

Brown, H. (2016). English-medium instruction in Japan: Discussing implications for language teaching. In P. Clements, A. Krause, & H. Brown (Eds.). *Focus on the learner*. JALT.

Brown, H. (2018). *Getting started with English-medium instruction in Japan: key factors in program planning and implementation*. Unpublished doctoral dissertation: University of Birmingham.

Chapple, J. (2014). Finally feasible or fresh façade? Analysing the internationalization plans of Japanese universities. *International Journal of Research Studies in Education, 3*(4), 15–28. https://doi.org/10.5861/ijrse.2014.794

Coleman, J. (2006). English-medium teaching in European higher education. *Language Teaching, 39*(1), 1–14. https://doi.org/10.1017/S026144480600320X

Costa, F. & Coleman, J. (2013). A survey of English-medium instruction in Italian higher education. *International Journal of Bilingual Education and Bilingualism, 16*(1), 3–19. https://doi.org/10.1080/13670050.2012.676621

de Jong, H. & Teekens, H. (2003). The case of the University of Twente: Internationalisation as education policy. *Journal of Studies in International Education, 7*(1), 41–51. https://doi.org/10.1177%2F1028315302250179

Dearden, J. (2014). *English as a medium of instruction - a growing global phenomenon*. British Council.

Education First (2017). *EF EPI The world's largest ranking of countries by English skills*. http://www.ef.edu/epi/

Enever, J. (2009). Languages, education and Europeanisation. In R. Dale & S. Robertson (Eds.). *Globalisation and Europeanisation in Education* (pp. 179–192). Symposium Books.

Galloway, N., Numajiri, T., & Rees, N. (2020). The 'internationalisation', or 'Englishisation', of higher education in East Asia. *Higher Education, 80*, 395–414. https://doi.org/10.1007/s10734-019-00486-1

Galloway, N. & Ruegg, R. (2020). The provision of student support on English Medium Instruction programmes in Japan and China. *Journal of English for Academic Purposes, 45*. https://doi.org/10.1016/j.jeap.2020.100846

Hellekjaer, G. (2010). Lecture comprehension in English-medium higher education. *Journal of Language and Communication Studies, 45*, 11–34. https://doi.org/10.7146/hjlcb.v23i45.97343

Hennings, M. & Mintz, S. (2015). Japan's measures to attract international students and the impact of student mobility on the labor market. *Journal of International and Advanced Japanese Studies, 7*, 241–251.

Ishikura, Y. (2015). Realizing internationalization at home through English-medium courses at a Japanese university: Strategies to maximize student learning. *Higher Learning Research Communications, 5*(1), 11–28. http://hdl.handle.net/11268/4645

Japan Times (2019, April 16). *English levels at Japan's secondary schools falls short of government target*. https://www.japantimes.co.jp/news/2019/04/16/national/english-level-japans-secondary-schools-falls-short-government-target/

Kachru, B. (1982). *The other tongue: English across cultures*. University of Illinois Press.

Kelo, M., Rogers, T. (with Rumbley, L.) (2010). International student support in European Higher Education: Needs, solutions and challenges. *ACA Papers on International Cooperation in Education*. Lemmens.

Kitahama, H. (2003). A consideration of the short-term exchange program in Japan: Its present problems and future trends – Evidence from application in Osaka University. *Ryugakusei Kyouiku* [International student education], 8, 53–78.

Kojima, N. (2016, November 26). *Student motivation and challenges in EMI lectures*. Paper presented at the Japan Association of Language Teaching Conference, Nagoya, Japan.

Lassegard, J. (2006). International student quality and Japanese higher education reform. *Journal of Studies in International Education*, 10(2), 119–140. https://doi.org/10.1177%2F1028315305283878

Leask, B. (2009). Using formal and informal curricula to improve interactions between home and international students. *Journal of Studies in International Education*, 13(2), 205–221. https://doi.org/10.1177%2F1028315308329786

MEXT (n.d.a). *Project for promotion of global human resource development*. http://www.mext.go.jp/en/policy/education/highered/title02/detail02/sdetail02/1373895.htm

MEXT (n.d.b). *Top global university project*. https://www.mext.go.jp/en/policy/education/highered/title02/detail02/sdetail02/1395420.htm

MEXT (2011). *Daigaku ni okeru kyoiku naiyo to-no kaikaku jokyo-ni tsuite (Heisei 23 nendono)*. [Status of the reform of educational contents at universities: 2011 survey results.] http://www.mext.go.jp/a_menu/koutou/daigaku/04052801/1341433.htm

MEXT (2015). *Overseas study by Japanese nationals*. http://www.mext.go.jp/en/news/topics/detail/__icsFiles/afieldfile/2015/05/08/1357495_01.pdf

MEXT (2016a). *Heisei 27 nenndo eigokyoiku jisshi jyokyo chousa*. [Investigation of English Education in 2015.] from: http://www.mext.go.jp/component/a_menu/education/detail/__icsFiles/afieldfile/2016/04/05/1369254_3_1.pdf

MEXT (2016b). *Statistical abstract 2016 edition: Universities and junior colleges*. http://www.mext.go.jp/en/publication/statistics/title02/detail02/1379369.htm

MEXT (2019). *Heisei 28 nendono daigaku ni okeru kyoiku naiyo to-no kaikaku jokyo-ni tsuite (gaiyo)*. [2016 Reform status of educational content at universities: Overview]. https://www.mext.go.jp/a_menu/koutou/daigaku/04052801/__icsFiles/afieldfile/2019/05/28/1417336_001.pdf

Morais, D. B. & Ogden, A. C. (2011). Initial development and validation of the global citizenship scale. *Journal of Studies in International Education*, 15(5), 445–466. https://doi.org/10.1177/1028315310375308

Morita, L. (2015). English, language shift and values shift in Japan and Singapore. *Globalization, Societies and Education*, 13(4), 508–527. https://doi.org/10.1080/14767724.2014.967184

Morizumi, F. (2015). EMI in Japan: Current status and its implications. *Educational Studies*, 57, 119–128.

Nastansky, H. L. (2004). National strategy in the internationalisation of higher education: The German perspective. In R. Wilkinson (Ed.). *Integrating content and language: Meeting the challenge of a multilingual higher education* (pp. 49–54). Universitaire.
Nikkei Asian Review (2016, April 5). *Many of Japan's English teachers miss proficiency benchmark*. http://asia.nikkei.com/Life-Arts/Education/Many-of-Japan-s-English-teachers-miss-proficiency-benchmark
OECD (2016). *Education at a glance 2016: OECD indicators.* OECD Publishing.
Phillipson, R. (2009). *Linguistic imperialism continued.* Taylor and Francis.
Röemer, A. (2002). A more valid alternative to TOEFL? *College and University, 77*(4), 13–17.
Taguchi, N. (2005). The communicative approach in Japanese secondary schools: Teachers' perceptions and practice. *The Language Teacher, 29*(3), 3–9.
Takagi, H. (2009). Internationalization of undergraduate curricula: The gap between ideas and practice in Japan. *London Review of Education, 7*(1), 31–39. https://doi.org/10.1080/14748460802700603
Tardy, C. (2004). The role of English in scientific communication: Lingus Franca or Tyrannosaurus Rex? *Journal of English for Academic Purposes, 3*, 247–269. https://doi.org/10.1016/j.jeap.2003.10.001
Toh, G. (2014). English for content instruction in a Japanese higher education setting: examining challenges, contradictions and anomalies. *Language and Education, 28*(4), 299–318. https://doi.org/10.1080/09500782.2013.857348
Tsuneyoshi, R. (2005). Internationalization strategies in Japan: The dilemmas and possibilities of study abroad programs using English. *Journal of Research in International Education, 4*(1), 65–86. https://doi.org/10.1177%2F1475240905050291
Van der Wende, M. C. (2000). Internationalizing the curriculum: New perspectives and challenges. In B. Hudson & M. J. Todds (Eds.). *Internationalizing the curriculum in higher education.* Sheffeld Hallam University Press.
Vinke, A. (1995). *English as a medium of instruction in Dutch engineering education.* Unpublished PhD dissertation: Delft University of Technology.
Wächter, B. & Maiworm, F. (2015). English-taught programmes in European higher education: The state of play in 2014. *ACA papers on international cooperation in education.* Lemmens.
Wächter, B. & Maiworm, F. (2008). English-taught programmes in European higher education. *ACA papers on international cooperation in education.* Lemmens.
Wilkinson, R. (2005). *The impact of language on teaching content: Views from the content teacher.* Paper presented at the Bi- and Multi-lingual universities – Challenges and future prospects Conference, Helsinki, Finland. http://www.palmenia.helsinki.fi/congress/bilingual2005/presentations/wilkinson.pdf
Wilkinson, R. (2013). English-medium Instruction at a Dutch university: Challenges and pitfalls. In A. Doiz, D. Lasagabaster, & J. M. Sierra (Eds.). *English-medium instruction at universities: Global challenges.* Multilingual Matters.

2 Initiatives for student support in full-degree EMI programmes in Japan

Background

Some would argue that support should be offered outside of the classroom to help students succeed in any educational institution. Most would agree that support for students is required in the tertiary EMI context, due to additional challenges posed to students in this context. As mentioned in the introductory chapter, the multicultural and multilingual composition of the student body in the average ETP cause difficulties for students. Especially, differences in content knowledge of students from different educational backgrounds and differences in language proficiency levels cause serious challenges to a large number of students in this context. Ideally, there should be support available to students outside of the classroom to help them overcome these challenges and successfully progress through the curriculum.

Even in cases in which a student has the requisite background content knowledge and a suitable level of language proficiency, some of the challenges for faculty mentioned in the introductory chapter can lead to difficulties for students. For example, faculty may lack cross-cultural awareness or pedagogical awareness. In either case, although the faculty member is knowledgeable in their content area and highly proficient in English, they may fail to get through to students. Previous researchers have found that a lack of cross-cultural awareness (Kelo & Rogers, 2010; Leask, 2009) or pedagogical awareness (Lassegard, 2006) can cause challenges for students. Providing support for students outside of the classroom can help even academically and linguistically well-prepared students to overcome these challenges.

It would be wonderful to believe that all faculty at all universities have sufficient time to interact one-to-one with students, but in reality faculty at most universities are busy and it is not easy to find the time for extensive one-to-one work with students. As Tsuneyoshi (2005) mentioned, in some cases, faculty in Japan are not compensated for the additional time spent preparing to teach content in English; instead, EMI classes may be added as a "voluntary" contribution over and above the usual workload. In this case, faculty may be exceptionally busy and have very little time to interact with students outside of the classroom. This is one rationale for offering additional support to students outside of the teacher-student relationship.

Another aspect suggesting additional support should be available outside of the teacher-student relationship is the concept of learner autonomy. Learner autonomy is based on the ancient idea that if you give someone a fish, you can feed them for a day, but if you teach them how to fish, you can feed them for a lifetime. Educators interested in promoting learner autonomy would focus more on skills and learning strategies that can be applied in future contexts, rather than only teaching them facts. If an institution values the idea of students learning to become better learners, rather than just learning content, then offering support to students outside of the teacher-student relationship can help students to become better learners. Students going outside of the teacher-student relationship for help can be the first step in the process of becoming less dependent on the classroom teacher and more autonomous. This bodes well for developing graduates who are capable of working autonomously.

To help students overcome differences in their educational background, alleviate problems caused by teachers' lack of cross-cultural communication skills or pedagogical skills, and/or to develop students who are able to work autonomously, support should be offered to students outside of the teacher-student relationship in the EMI context. This support could take many different forms and serve many different purposes. The purpose of this chapter is to present an overview of the kinds of support offered to students outside of the teacher-student relationship in the context of EMI full degree programmes/departments in Japan.

Incentives for offering student support

In a large-scale study conducted in the United States (Kuh et al., 2010), five groups of desirable educational practices were identified that distinguish universities and colleges that are academically effective from those that are not. One of the groups of practices that predicted educational effectiveness was a supportive campus environment. A supportive campus environment is an environment in which support is available to students to help them succeed. The educational effectiveness of a supportive campus environment may be the main incentive for all tertiary education institutions to set up academic support services for students.

Another of the groups of desirable educational practices identified by Kuh et al. (2010) was academic challenge. This will come as no surprise to educational assessment specialists, as past research in the field has found that academic challenge, in the form of high expectations and strict assessment practices has been found to predict increased academic achievement (Betts & Grogger, 2003; Bonesronning, 2004; Figlio & Lucas, 2004). However, while challenge is necessary, it is not sufficient to enable academic success. Bennett (1993) posits that there needs to be a good balance between the amount of challenge and that of support. That is; challenge pushes students to go beyond what they are already confidently capable of, but support enables them to reach that next level. According to Bennett (1993), if students are challenged too much without enough support, it will be difficult for them to succeed. However, if they are not challenged enough, it will be difficult for them to maintain motivation. Therefore, a suitable level of academic challenge and a suitable level of support need to be combined to create an ideal environment for academic success. Lassegard (2006) suggests more specifically that multifaceted extra-curricular support is necessary for students who struggle with either language or academic issues to succeed.

Research on student support outside of Japan

In the context of European higher education, Kelo (2006) identified four different beliefs about support held by those employed in educational institutions. The participants either believed that 1) all students require a lot of support, regardless of their personal characteristics, that 2) international students have a different/more/more immediate need for support, that 3) each individual should be treated as such, having different needs regardless of whether they are international or domestic students or that 4) international students and domestic students should be treated the same and offered the same support options. It has commonly been found that international students tended to use support services at higher rates than domestic students (Cross et al., 2015; Williams & Takaku, 2011). These views of educators and research results suggest that in a context with a large number of international students, the need for support may be higher than in a more monocultural context.

Leask (2009) focussed on the support for students offered in a university in Australia with a large number of international students. She suggested that student support (the "informal curriculum") should be closely aligned to the formal curriculum taught in the classroom. She also stressed that if an institution hopes to be international, then internationalisation should be a part of both the formal and the informal curriculum. Since one of the main aims of ETPs is internationalisation, it is clear that not only the formal but also the informal curriculum should be internationalised. However, how exactly the internationalisation of the informal curriculum can best be achieved is less clear.

One of the biggest difficulties facing international students is considered to be insufficient language proficiency (Kelo, 2006; Leask, 2009). Thus, language proficiency related support should be one of the highest priorities when offering support to international students. However, in the context of European EMI, it was found that "Students with language difficulties also have culturally-related problems" (Kelo, 2006, p. 171). Kelo suggests that cultural differences in learning methods should be ameliorated by introducing international students to local learning methods. For example, Kelo and Rogers (2010) mention that students may be unfamiliar with learning in a workshop style, instead of being used to attending lectures, and in some cultural contexts, there may be more emphasis on independent learning, whereas in others more structure may be provided by instructors. In addition to learning methods, in cases where the international students come from very different cultural backgrounds from that of the university, it would seem necessary to also introduce the international students to the expectations upon them in the host educational culture.

Kelo and Rogers (2010) also investigated the types of support offered in the European context and perceptions of the support services provided. They identified various kinds of support offered by institutions in Europe, including study skills workshops, individual tutoring, on-demand workshops and self-access centres. However, support for the teaching language was often not offered at all. In most cases, institutions set English language proficiency requirements as a part of the admissions process and assumed that students who met the requirements did not require English language support after arrival (Kelo & Rogers, 2010); instead, they mainly offered language support in the local language. In practice, even when second language learners have achieved the requisite language proficiency score to enter a university programme, this does not guarantee that they have sufficient English language skills to succeed in the EMI context (Bradford, 2013; Kelo & Rogers, 2010; Röemer, 2002). Therefore, it may be misguided for institutions not to offer English language support to students in the EMI context, even if strict English proficiency test scores are required to enter the programme.

In addition to what kind of support services are offered, another consideration is who the support services are available to. Kelo (2006) found that degree-seeking international students tended to have the same support services available to them that degree-seeking domestic students had. However, she also found that short-term international exchange students tended to be provided with more support than degree-seeking students. The main support services that students in Europe reported being available to them were "Library and research support (83%), Support for academic problems (55%), Language support (47%), and Individual academic tutoring (40%)" (Kelo & Rogers, 2010, p. 67).

In terms of students' perceptions of their need for support services, Kelo and Rogers (2010) collected survey responses from 1278 degree-seeking students from outside of Europe, who were studying in European universities. The students ranked different kinds of support in the following way: Support for academic problems was considered to be the most important, followed by library and research support, individual academic tutoring, and language support. Another study (The Council for International Education (UKCOSA), 2004) found that 75% of undergraduate students were satisfied or very satisfied with the academic support offered at universities in the United Kingdom. The study also found higher uptake of study skills support than language support, as well as higher levels of satisfaction with study skills support than language support.

Little is known about the relationship between the need for services and uptake as well as between uptake and cultural and individual differences (Kelo & Rogers, 2010). What is clear though is the connection between tuition fees and services expected by students. The more an institution charges the more value they need to offer to students in order to satisfy them. Indeed, Kelo (2006) found that the more tuition a university charged to international students, the more extensive support services they provided. The OECD (2016) reported that full-time undergraduate students in Japan were second only to the United States in terms of the average tuition paid. This being the case, we could expect that students in Japan would be provided with very extensive support services to help them succeed in their studies. One of the purposes of this study is to find out whether this is the case.

Student support in the Japanese context

In 2005, Tsuneyoshi reported that there was no systematic support offered to Japanese students at the University of Tokyo if they had difficulties succeeding in English-medium classes. While some support was offered to international students, it was Japanese language help rather than English language support, and even the amount of Japanese support offered was minimal (Tsuneyoshi, 2005). This may come as a surprise to some as the University of Tokyo is considered to be one of the universities in Japan with the highest educational standards. Furthermore, there is evidence that at some other universities in Japan, support was being offered to students before this time. For example, International Student Advisors (ISAs) are professional support staff members employed to provide support and tutoring to international students (Lassegard, 2006). However, he also reports that the existence of an ISA within a faculty depends on the number of international students in the department and ISAs are also offered at the discretion of the faculty. These two factors mean that in many cases, there are no ISAs even when international students are present. However, a tutoring system is in place at all national universities, in which each international degree-seeking student is matched with a domestic graduate student who is expected to offer academic support, such as subject-based tutoring and exam preparation help (Lassegard, 2006). In reality, the tutors are often used for help with daily life rather than with academic matters. Overall, Lassegard (2006) reports major disparities between universities and departments in terms of the support offered in the Japanese higher education context.

Bradford (2013) agrees that despite having met English proficiency benchmarks for entry into an EMI programme, students still require language and academic skills support and suggests that one way to do this is through the foundation and/or use of a writing centre. The number of writing centres in Japan seems to have been increasing from around 2004, when many of the current writing centres were founded (i.e. Osaka Jogakuin University, Kanda University of International Studies, Sophia University, Waseda University). As at the 2013 academic year, my colleagues and I were able to find 24 universities in Japan offering support for writing and/or other academic skills in English medium.

Clearly, providing support to students does not guarantee that they will use that support, even if they need support to succeed. Ishikura (2015) distributed a questionnaire to all students at one university who were not enrolled in an ETP but were taking English-medium courses. She found that 30% of international students found the EMI courses they were taking "difficult" or "too difficult" and 28% reported a need for support. On the other hand, when it came to Japanese domestic students, more students found the EMI courses "difficult" or "too difficult" but less reported a need for support. Ishikura (2015) concluded that a lower retention rate of Japanese domestic students in EMI courses is partly a result of their lower uptake of available support.

It is apparent that support is offered at some universities in Japan. However, previous research has not provided an overview of the different kinds of support offered throughout Japan. The purpose of the study reported in this chapter is to provide an overview of the kinds of support offered to students within English Taught Programmes (ETPs) in Japan. Given the famously low language proficiency levels in Japan (e.g. Morita, 2015; Tsuneyoshi, 2005) and the relatively high cost of tertiary tuition in Japan (Second only to the United States, according to OECD, 2016), it is expected that extensive support is offered to students to help them succeed in their English-medium studies.

Support offerings in ETPs in Japan

A questionnaire was developed to illuminate the details of the student support offerings in ETPS in Japan. The first section (four questions) gathered background information about the institutions. Question five asked whether any systematic support was available to students who were studying in the English medium, excluding any support offered within the teacher-student relationship. The remainder of the questionnaire (nine questions) asked details of the support system present, such as who can receive the support, when and for how long, who provides the support, the language used in the provision of the support and whether the support was optional or compulsory. The questionnaire can be seen in Appendix A.

MEXT (2011) identified 16 universities offering ETPs in Japan. However, one of the universities identified (Miyazaki International College) does not meet the MEXT definition of EMI. Although students at Miyazaki International College take content classes in the medium of English and the classes are team-taught by a content area specialist and a language educator, outcomes of the programme are measured based on students' English proficiency test scores. There are no attempts to measure the content knowledge outcomes of the programme and it is, therefore, apparent that the primary aim of the programme is language education. In effect, Miyazaki International College is a form of Content Based Learning, a common approach to teaching language, innovatively introduced in a whole degree format.

The other 15 universities identified by MEXT (2011) were invited to participate in this research. The 15 universities on this list were:

- Akita International University
- Hosei University
- International Christian University
- Kwansei Gakuin University
- Kyoto University
- Kyushu University
- Meiji Gakuin University
- Meiji University
- Nagoya University
- Ritsumeikan Asia Pacific University
- Ritsumeikan University
- Sophia University
- Tama University
- Tohoku University
- Waseda University

In addition to these 15 universities, the author identified an additional eight universities offering ETPs in Japan and contacted them to request their participation in the survey. They were:

- Doshisha University
- Keio University
- Osaka University
- Rikkyo University
- Soka University
- The University of Tokyo
- University of Tsukuba
- Yamanashi Gakuin University

The participants who received a link to the questionnaire by e-mail included one faculty member at each of the 23 ETPs identified. On some of the university websites, it was possible to identify who was most likely to be in charge of matters such as student support and these faculty members were contacted. On some of the university websites, no detailed information about individual faculty or staff was offered. In these cases, the researcher relied on finding faculty members who had previously published on the topic or identifying the more appropriate participant through known contacts employed at each university. When this was impossible, an e-mail was sent to a generic administrative e-mail address

32 *Initiatives for student support*

for the department in question, with a request to forward the link on to the most appropriate faculty or staff member.

Participants were given one month to complete the questionnaire. However, they received a reminder e-mail two weeks prior to the questionnaire closing date, in addition to one week prior to the date. This process resulted in 22 of the 23 potential participants starting to answer the questionnaire (a response rate of 96%). However, ultimately only 18 participants completed the entire questionnaire (a response rate of 78%).

Twenty-two participants answered question one, which sought confirmation that their university had an ETP. The question asked: "For the purpose of this research, an EMI program/department is defined as a program/department in which all the classes that a student needs to graduate are offered in English. Please confirm that this was the case at your university as of the 2016 academic year." Nineteen participants answered "yes", while three answered "no". On the basis of these responses, there appear to be nineteen or twenty universities in Japan offering at least one ETP. It is also possible that the number might be slightly higher as there may be EMI programmes/departments that were not included in this research.

Seventeen of the nineteen participants who answered "yes" to question one responded to question two, which asked how long the university had been offering EMI programs. A possible reason for this is that some participants may not know when the EMI programme began. The results can be seen in Figure 2.1. The results were almost evenly divided between having offered an EMI programme for seven years or more (since 2010 or earlier) and having offered one for six years or less (since 2011 or later). The number of participants who chose the former being just one more than the number who chose the latter.

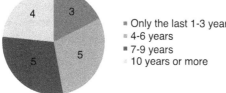

Figure 2.1 Age of EMI programmes.

Initiatives for student support 33

All nineteen participants at ETP offering universities responded to question three. As can be seen in Figure 2.2, no-one responded that language education was the dominant purpose of EMI instruction at their institutions. This is in contrast to the finding of Brown (2016). In his research, improving the language proficiency of Japanese students was reported to be one of the most important aims of EMI programmes in Japan. However, Brown's (2016) participants were mainly offering ad hoc EMI (EMI classes within a programme taught in Japanese) rather than ETPs. This may be one of the main differences between ad hoc EMI and ETPs. Seven participants answered that the EMI instruction was intended to achieve both language education and subject learning, while 12 answered that the dominant purpose was subject learning. Some differences were found between the responses to other questions of those who answered that the purpose was both language education and subject learning and those who answered that the dominant purpose was subject learning.

Of the nineteen participants employed at universities with ETPs, eighteen answered question four, which asked about the proportion of Japanese domestic students in the ETP. As can be seen in Figure 2.3, the answers were evenly divided between those who estimated that between one and twenty per cent of the students in the programme were Japanese domestic students and those who answered that somewhere between 41% and 99% were Japanese domestic students, with the smallest number of the latter group choosing 41–60%. Thus, two groups of programmes are apparent: those targeting and/or attracting mainly international students and those targeting and/or attracting mainly Japanese domestic students.

Fifteen of the participants at ETP offering universities responded to question five, which asked whether any systematic support was offered

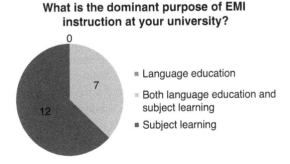

Figure 2.2 Dominant purpose of EMI instruction.

34 *Initiatives for student support*

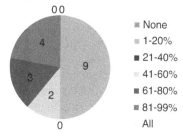

Figure 2.3 Percentage of Japanese domestic students.

outside of the classroom. Twelve (80%) responded that some form of systematic support was offered outside of the classroom by someone other than the classroom teacher, while the remaining three (20%) answered that no systematic support was offered outside of the classroom by anyone other than the classroom teacher. Interestingly, all three participants who responded that no systematic support was offered outside of the classroom also responded that the dominant purpose of the EMI instruction was subject learning, whereas at all of the institutions who offer EMI both for the purpose of language education and subject learning systematic support is offered outside of the classroom.

Further analysis indicated that the longer an EMI programme had been in operation, the more likely they were to offer support to students. This relationship can be seen in Figure 2.4. At all of the universities which had been offering an EMI programme for ten years or more, some form of support was offered to students. On the other hand, the universities where an EMI programme had been offered for only one to three years were only half as likely to offer support. This suggests that programmes found support to be necessary after their establishment and added support for students at a later date. New programmes could learn from the experience of more established departments and consider setting up a student support mechanism from the outset to enhance the success of the programme.

All 12 of the participants who answered that systematic support is offered outside of the classroom also indicated which types of

Initiatives for student support 35

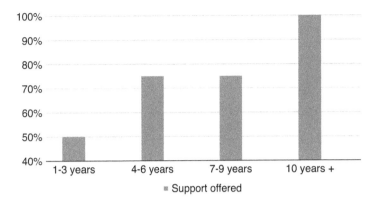

Figure 2.4 Relationship between age of programme and support offered.

systematic support are offered. As can be seen in Figure 2.5, writing skills support is the most commonly offered, being offered by eight of the 12 institutions. This is followed by the existence of a self-access centre, at which students can undertake self-directed study (although often with support from others, as will be discussed later in this section). Half of the respondents (6) responded that their institution has a self-access centre. The next most frequently offered support is speaking and listening skills support. One-third of the participants (4) answered that this kind of support is offered at their institutions. The least frequently offered support was reading support, which was offered at

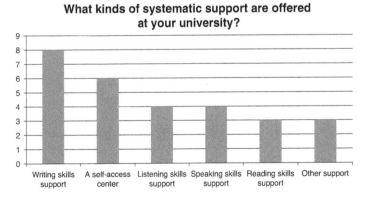

Figure 2.5 Types of support offered.

just three of the institutions. Two of these institutions had established their programmes ten years ago or more, while the other one had been established seven to nine years ago. At the institution that will be the focus of the next chapter, through time both instructors and students expressed the need for reading support and reading support was added to the support services on offer in order to fill that need. This result suggests that something similar may have occurred at other universities. It is suggested that newer EMI programmes follow this lead and introduce reading support sooner rather than later in order to prevent difficulties for students caused by a lack of academic reading skills.

Reading support may be offered less often on the basis that it is the main focus of English language education at the junior high school and high school levels in Japan. However, it would seem unwise not to offer reading support to students attending classes which require reading to be done in English, since reading is the primary means through which students receive knowledge in tertiary level content classes.

Three respondents also selected "other support". They explained that support is offered to prepare students for English language proficiency tests, such as TOEFL, and IELTS, that intensive workshops are offered on other academic skills, such as presentation and technical writing, that research workshops are run by library staff, and a conversation café is offered, where students can go to practice speaking and listening.

Of the 12 participants who answered that support outside of the classroom is available, 11 provided a response to question seven: "In which language is the support offered?" Two answered that support is offered in English, while the remaining nine answered that support is offered in both Japanese and English. No participants reported support being offered only in Japanese.

Question eight asked who such support was available to and was also answered by eleven participants. As can be seen in Figure 2.6, both Japanese and international degree-seeking students could receive support at all of the institutions. However, there was one institution at which short-term international exchange students could not receive any additional support outside of the teacher-student relationship, despite it being offered to other types of students. This could be a result of funding for the support coming from a Ministry of Education, Culture, Sports, Science and Technology (MEXT) grant. In some cases, such taxpayer-funded grants are not permitted to be used to provide services to short-term visitors to Japan. In addition,

Initiatives for student support 37

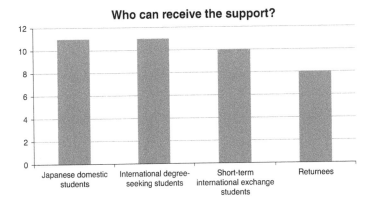

Figure 2.6 Who can receive support?

there were three institutions at which returnees could not receive support. This result suggests that there could be English proficiency levels above which students are not entitled to receive any support. This may be because of limitations in the capability of the support providers, such as the impression that since returnees are more fluent in English than those offering the support will not be effective for them. Alternatively, it may be considered by institutions that returnees are already competent in English and therefore do not require any support. However, Cummins (2008) suggested that five to seven years of education in an English-dominant environment would be required for an individual to achieve Cognitive Academic Language Proficiency. Many students considered to be returnees have only studied abroad for two to three years and many of them have studied in a language other than English. Furthermore, returnees are Japanese citizens and as such, they are entitled to the benefits of taxpayer-funded grants. Therefore, returnees should have access to the same support services as other degree-seeking students.

Eleven of the participants at institutions offering support outside of the classroom also responded to question nine, which asked who provided that support. The responses to question nine can be seen in Figure 2.7. The responses ranged from instructors at the universities, which was the most frequent response, to international postgraduate students, international undergraduate students, dedicated learning support staff, Japanese undergraduate students and Japanese postgraduate students. One interesting finding is the popularity of using

38 Initiatives for student support

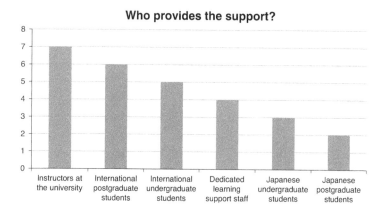

Figure 2.7 Who provides the support?

non-Japanese students to provide support. Another interesting observation is that Japanese undergraduate students are used in the provision of support more than Japanese postgraduate students, whereas the opposite is true for international students.

Differences were apparent between the purpose of EMI instruction and who provides support. At the institutions where EMI is conducted both for the purpose of language education and subject learning, no Japanese students (neither undergraduate nor postgraduate) provide support and support was reported to be offered more often by international students (5) than by faculty or dedicated learning support staff (4). At the institutions where EMI is offered for the purpose of subject learning, on the other hand, the responses were more balanced between international students (6) and Japanese students (5) and between undergraduate students (5) and postgraduate students (6) as well as being more balanced between faculty or dedicated learning support staff (7) and students (11).

Eleven of the 12 participants who responded that their institutions offer systematic support outside of the classroom also described the kinds of support offered in response to question 10, "In your own words, please describe the kind of systematic support offered outside of the classroom at your university." One participant answered that the support offered was "Token and shallow", elaborating that the staff who offer the support do not speak English. This was an institution at which less than 20% of the students are Japanese domestic students, so it does seem that English proficiency would be a prerequisite if the support is to help international students to succeed.

One participant responded that there was a conversation lounge at the university. As you may recall, a participant at a different university responded that there was a conversation café, as an explanation of "other" in question six. Therefore, there are two universities offering this kind of support. At both of these institutions, the purpose of EMI instruction is both language education and subject learning, and the conversation lounge/café seems to support the language learning function.

One participant mentioned that students are required to offer support as partial credit for a Second Language Acquisition course, which mainly international students take. In that course, the types of activities carried out vary through time, but individual peer tutoring was mentioned as one of the activities carried out. Similarly, two other participants mentioned buddy systems in which international students and Japanese students are paired together to support each other academically.

Two participants mentioned peer and/or professional learning advisors who work within the self-access centres at their institutions. They go by different names but offer similar kinds of advice. For example, recommending materials and study methods that may be effective for students to reach their goals.

Finally, six participants mentioned support in the style of a writing centre. Two mentioned specifically that peers offered the support and three mentioned that writing centre-style tutorials were offered by faculty and/or professional tutors. Overall, this writing centre-style of support was the most common response.

Eleven of the participants who responded that their institutions offer systematic support also answered question eleven, which asked about the frequency of students being able to receive such support. As can be seen in Figure 2.8, a similar number of participants responded that students could receive support seven times or more per week and that students could receive support two to four times a week. In addition to these responses, one participant answered that support is offered just a few times per semester and three elaborated that students can receive support without limit.

Ten of the 12 participants who responded that systematic support is offered within their institution answered question 12, which asked about the duration of support sessions. As can be seen in Figure 2.9, at a majority of universities, support is offered for periods of up to one hour (80%). Support is offered for longer periods at a minority of institutions (20%) and no institution offered support for periods of longer than two hours. In addition to these responses, one participant mentioned that

40 *Initiatives for student support*

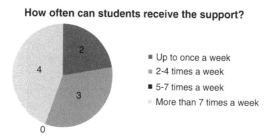

Figure 2.8 How often can students receive support?

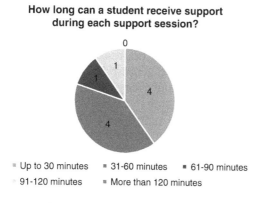

Figure 2.9 Length of each support session.

students could receive support for periods ranging from 30 minutes to 90 minutes, depending on their needs. At nine of the responding universities, support is available to students throughout their undergraduate studies, while at two institutions students can receive support only in the first year.

A point made by one of the respondents was that offering support depends upon funds being available to pay for that support. The respondent mentioned that sometimes funding comes in the form of a MEXT grant, but when the grant term ends the funding becomes unavailable and therefore, the support cannot always be continued. If institutions feel that the initiatives they have started with grant funding are valuable, then they will need to find a funding mechanism in order to continue the initiatives once the grant period is over. It would seem that this is easier for a private university to manage than for a public university. Furthermore, as students in private universities pay a great deal more tuition than those in public universities, there may be a correlated expectation of more support being available there. On the other hand, in publicly funded universities, funding levels have been decreasing year by year as the national population decreases. Thus, it is becoming increasingly difficult to find alternative funding mechanisms. Therefore, it is increasingly difficult to maintain aspects of the university, such as student support services, which some could consider unnecessary.

Eleven respondents answered question 14, which asked whether support was compulsory. At one university, students are required to attend one support session in the writing centre, after which the service is completely optional. This practice is also commonly used in North American university writing centres with the purpose of ensuring that students know about the support on offer. The idea is that once they have experienced the support once they will have a deeper understanding of what the support is like and it is thus more likely that they will consider using the service again at a later stage. At the remaining ten universities, the support services are completely optional, although it is not unusual that classroom teachers strongly recommend the use of the support services.

Another interesting point mentioned by one respondent was that, although the use of the support services is completely optional, offering such support services was compulsory for the university. At that university, a new EMI programme has been started in the last one to three years and is currently in a four-year probationary period. During this period the university is required by MEXT to provide support to students.

The current situation in ETPs in Japan

Since the purpose of this chapter is to provide an overview of support offered to students within Japanese ETPs, this section will make some estimates about the situation in Japanese ETPs as a whole on the basis of the questionnaire results collected. Clearly, not every ETP participated in the questionnaire (at least one institution offers an ETP but did not respond to the request to complete the questionnaire) and not all those who did respond answered every question (only 18 participants completed the entire questionnaire). Equally clearly, there are likely to be some aspects of student support that some of the respondents were unaware of and/or failed to mention, although they exist at their university. These are all limitations at play with questionnaire data. With these caveats in mind, this section will attempt to provide the bigger picture, a summary of support offered at ETPs in the Japanese context.

The author identified 23 possible ETPs in Japan. Three of these candidates responded that their university does not offer a programme from which a student can graduate after only having taken classes in English. Therefore, it is estimated that there are 19 or 20 ETPs in Japan, as of the 2016 academic year, and this number is increasing as time goes on.

Japanese domestic students constitute between one third and a half of all students in ETPs in Japan. Based on the results of this research, it is estimated that, overall, around 40% of the students in Japanese ETPs are Japanese domestic students. This result makes it seem fairly unlikely that very many EMI classes within ETPs would consist of only Japanese domestic students, which in turn provides a very real necessity for instructors to use English as the sole medium of instruction, including all class readings and assignments. Although many students choose to study in Japan partly or wholly to learn the Japanese language, those kinds of students have many bilingual and monolingual Japanese-medium programmes available to them in Japan, so it seems unlikely that they would choose to enrol in an ETP.

In the range of 60% to 90% of the ETPs in Japan offer some kind of support to students to help them succeed academically. However, it is estimated that 63% (12 out of 19 ETPs) do so. The older an ETP is, the more likely the institution is to offer some form of student support. The probability of an ETP offering support for academic writing is just slightly more than 50-50. At an average ETP, no support will be offered beyond writing support. This supports Kelo and Rogers's (2010) finding that in the European EMI context, support for academic writing is a great deal more common than other forms of support.

Support is more likely to be offered in both Japanese and English than only in English. Further analysis found that six of the nine participants who responded that support is offered in both Japanese and English reported that the proportion of Japanese domestic students in the ETP was just one to 20%. Of the institutions which have between 41% and 99% Japanese domestic students in their EMI programmes, two offer support in English only and three offer support in both Japanese and English.

There are a lot of variables influencing the language in which support is offered. Most often, in an ETP English is the only common language (the only language in which all parties are minimally proficient). However, as mentioned by one participant, despite the ETP being composed of mainly international students (at least 80%), the support staff at their institution cannot speak English and therefore the support provided is not very useful. In some cases, institutions find it difficult to recruit professional support staff who have sufficient English language proficiency in providing effective support in English. This would seem to suggest that universities should employ successful students as providers of support, rather than relying on professional support staff, especially outside of the main metropolitan areas, where it may be difficult to attract enough staff with sufficient English language proficiency.

Another aspect of the language issue which was not elucidated through this questionnaire was the mechanism through which the provision of support in both Japanese and English is controlled. For example, it may be that different providers offer support in different languages, based on their language competencies. It may be that there is an English-only policy, but in practice, providers provide support in both languages because of insufficient proficiency levels of the students who receive support. When the support is provided in the form of a buddy system, whereby an international student is matched with a domestic student, there may be a bilingual policy, by which each provides support in their own dominant language. As each institutional context is unique, it is expected that not only their policies but also the reasons for their policies and practices will vary in accord with contextual variables.

When considering the length and frequency of support offerings at institutions where support is offered, the average ETP offers support between 30 minutes and one hour per session. The average frequency of support offerings is between four and six times a week; on average, students can receive up to four sessions per week throughout their four years (or more) of undergraduate study. This would amount to three hours of support per week being offered to each individual student, on average. However, it must be considered that the support offered is optional, or mostly optional, in all institutions included in this study. Although receiving support is often strongly encouraged by classroom teachers, it is to be expected that the actual number of students who partake in such support services is a small proportion of the students enrolled in such programmes.

It is fair to say that overall, the support offerings at Japanese universities offering ETPs do not seem insufficient. However, we should keep in mind that the tuition paid by Japanese students is second only to that paid in the United States (OECD, 2016). Therefore, it is not unreasonable to expect more than is currently offered in many institutions. In particular, an estimated 37% of institutions offering ETPs in Japan do not offer any support to students outside of the teacher-student relationship (seven out of 19 ETPs). Providing no support for students leads to one of two results. It may burden classroom teachers with the need for one-to-one work with individual students outside of the classroom, which in turn may lead to a lack of time for course preparation, planning and feedback provision, and thus may reduce the quality of the educational offerings. Alternatively, a lack of support will necessitate a curriculum that does not challenge students, thus reducing the quality of the educational offerings. According to Bennett (1993), if students are not challenged enough, this will make it difficult for them to maintain motivation for learning. Evidence relating to Japanese universities more generally suggests that the latter may often be the case (Horie, 2003; Igami, 2014; McVeigh, 2002).

Apart from the institutions at which support is not offered to students in ETPs, generally, the types of support offered appear to be fairly limited, and in particular, the number of programmes offering any form of reading support is small. Furthermore, there is a trend that programmes which have been established for longer are more likely to offer reading support than those that have been established more recently. It is hoped that knowing this trend may encourage newer programmes to recognise a need for reading support and add some form of reading support to their existing support offerings.

A number of institutions are offering peer support in Japan. For programmes that do not offer support or those that offer very limited support due to financial concerns, it is suggested that peer support may be an effective method of providing additional support in a cost-effective way. Several examples provided by participants in this chapter could be employed by those who are currently unable to offer (much) support. The most useful models mentioned by participants will be the reiterated here. A buddy system, in which international and Japanese students are paired together to help each other academically, would be very useful where funding is not available to pay for student support. In cases where there are very few international students, Japanese students could also be paired together to develop a form of PASS (Leask, 2009). Another possible variation would be to pair third-year students with first-year students, to create an official sempai-kohai academic support relationship. Another example which is useful in the case of a lack of funding is asking students to provide support for course credit. This could be carried out as part of an education-related course. For example, students in a teacher licensing programme could provide one-to-one, or small-group academic tutoring to others, such as first-year students, to help them achieve their academic goals. Although a lack of funding to pay for student support services does create a challenge for institutions, this challenge can be overcome with ingenuity.

References

Bennett, J. M. (1993). Cultural marginality: Identity issues in intercultural training. In R. M. Paige (Ed.). *Education for the intercultural experience* (pp. 109–135). Intercultural Press.

Betts, J. R. & Grogger, J. (2003). The impact of grading standards on student achievement, educational attainment, and entry-level earnings. *Economics of Education Review, 22*(4), 343–352. https://doi.org/10.1016/S0272-7757(02)00059-6

Bonesronning, H. (2004). Do the teachers' grading practices affect student achievement? *Education Economics, 12*(2), 151–167. https://doi.org/10.1080/0964529042000239168

Bradford, A. (2013). English-medium degree programs in Japanese universities: Learning from the European experience. *Asian Education and Development Studies, 2*(3), 225–240.

Brown, H. (2016). *English-medium instruction in Japan: Discussing implications for language teaching*. In P. Clements, A. Krause & H. Brown (Eds.). Focus on the Learner. JALT.

Cross, S., Holten, C., Picciotto, M., & Ruble, K. (2015). International students at the University of California: The impact on writing center practice. *CATESOL Journal, 27*(2), 73–87.

Cummins, J. (2008). Teaching for transfer: Challenging the two solitudes assumption in bilingual education. In J. Cummins & N. H. Hornberger (Eds.). *Encyclopedia of language and education* (pp. 65–75). Springer.

Figlio, D. N. & Lucas, M. E. (2004). Do high grading standards affect high performance? *Journal of Public Economics, 88*(9–10), 1815–1834. https://doi.org/10.1016/S0047-2727(03)00039-2

Horie, M. (2003). *International students and internationalization of higher education in Japan: Interpretive study with policy makers and international educators*. University of Minnesota.

Igami, K. (2014). Reform of university education for non-elite university students. *Japan Labor Review, 11*(2), 53–68.

Ishikura, Y. (2015). Realizing internationalization at home through English-medium courses at a Japanese university: Strategies to maximize student learning. *Higher Learning Research Communications, 5*(1), 11–28. http://hdl.handle.net/11268/4645

Kelo, M. (2006). Support for international students in higher education: Practice and principles. *ACA Papers on international cooperation in education*. Lemmens.

Kelo, M., & Rogers, T. (with Rumbley, L.) (2010). International student support in European Higher Education: Needs, solutions and challenges. *ACA papers on international cooperation in education*. Lemmens.

Kuh, G., Kinzie, J., Schuh, J., & Whitt, E. (and associates) (2010). *Student success in college: Creating conditions that matter*. Jossey Bass.

Lassegard, J. (2006). International student quality and Japanese higher education reform. *Journal of Studies in International Education, 10*(2), 119–140. https://doi.org/10.1177%2F1028315305283878

Leask, B. (2009). Using formal and informal curricula to improve interactions between home and international students. *Journal of Studies in International Education*, *13*(2), 205–221. https://doi.org/10.1177%2F1028315308329786

McVeigh, B. (2002). *Japanese higher education as myth*. M. E. Sharpe.

MEXT (2011). Daigaku ni okeru kyoiku naiyo to-no kaikaku jokyo-ni tsuite (Heisei 23 nendono). [Status of the reform of educational contents at universities: 2011 survey results.] http://www.mext.go.jp/a_menu/koutou/daigaku/04052801/1341433.html

Morita, L. (2015). English, language shift and values shift in Japan and Singapore. *Globalization, Societies and Education*, *13*(4), 508–527. https://doi.org/10.1080/14767724.2014.967184

OECD (2016). *Education at a glance 2016: OECD indicators*. OECD Publishing.

Röemer, A. (2002). A more valid alternative to TOEFL? *College and University*, *77*(4), 13–17.

The Council for International Education (UKCOSA) (2004). *Broadening our horizons: International students in UK universities and colleges*. Report of the UKCOSA survey.

Tsuneyoshi, R. (2005). Internationalization strategies in Japan: The dilemmas and possibilities of study abroad programs using English. *Journal of Research in International Education*, *4*(1), 65–86. https://doi.org/10.1177%2F1475240905050291

Williams, J. D. & Takaku, S. (2011). Help seeking, self-efficacy, and writing performance among college students. *Journal of Writing Research*, *3*(1), 1–18.

3 Case-study research investigating a support centre for EMI in Japan

Background

Establishing student support services requires a great deal of time, effort and resources (Schendel & Macauley, 2012). At the very least, a space is required, some furniture, at least one administrator and several paid or volunteer student or professional support staff. Beyond these basic resources, time is required to conceptualise and prepare for the student support offering/s. University administrators may be rightly concerned that if the decision is made to invest time, effort and resources into such an endeavour, there may be little demand for the support services and they may go unused. Therefore, evidence needs to be collected to assess the effectiveness of such a centre after its establishment.

The overriding purpose of any educational institution is the learning and development of students who enrol in the institution. Although there are differing opinions about the exact role of support services within a university, such as whether they should be remedial, to increase learner autonomy, or offer a form of extension for capable students, no-one is likely to disagree that the overriding purpose of such a support centre is student learning and development. In recent years, there has been an increased focus on assessing such services to determine both successes and areas in need of improvement in support service offerings.

The most straightforward approach to writing centre assessment is through the use of descriptive statistics, including usage rates and the number of hours of tutoring received by each student (Gofine, 2012). While numerous studies have investigated the usage of writing centres and academic support centres, this research has usually been conducted in contexts where the local language is also the language of instruction. Results of such studies do not necessarily generalise to EMI contexts where the majority of students are often non-native speakers of the medium of instruction and where the majority of students often share the same native language. Moreover, many such assessments have not gone beyond usage rates. Those that have gone beyond usage rates have rarely asked more than questions about user satisfaction. As suggested by Kalikoff (2001), Thompson (2006) and Gofine (2012), this chapter combines data from such questions with qualitative data obtained through open-ended questions.

In chapter two, it was discovered that peer support is relatively well employed within universities in Japan offering ETPs at which support is offered. Seventy-three per cent of the universities that reported offering any support reported offering some form of peer support. On the other hand, there was a noticeable preference to employ international students in 'peer' support positions and a related lack of employment of Japanese students. In the data presented in chapter two, only 12 institutions reported providing any support. Of those 12, only eight reported any support offered by peers (either international or domestic undergraduate or postgraduate students). Furthermore, of those eight institutions which reported offering any peer support, only three reported any peer support offered by Japanese domestic students. In the other five peer support offering institutions, peer support is offered exclusively by international students. There could be considered to be a certain contradiction in tutors fulfilling the roles of both peers and tutors at the same time (Trimbur, 1987). Furthermore, Harris (1992) suggests that when tutors are trained for the peer tutoring position, they stop being true peers and take on more of an educator role. The same argument could be made about employing international students as "peer" tutors in the Japanese context. Although many international students in Japanese universities are not native speakers of English, many universities specifically recruit native English speaking international students to deliver peer support. Thus, although they are peers in terms of being students at the same university, their international student status and, more importantly, their status as native speakers of English, places them in more of an expert role than that of a true peer. The decision to employ exclusively international students in peer support roles in 62% of the universities offering peer support would appear to be a form of "native-speakerism" (Holliday, 2006).

This chapter focusses on an academic support centre in an undergraduate ETP in Japan at which approximately 70% of the students are Japanese domestic students, 25% are short-term international exchange students and 5% are degree-seeking international students. The academic support centre under investigation was established at the beginning of the 2010 academic year. The centre employs peer tutors, who are paid to provide one-hour long one-to-one academic tutorial sessions in the centre. The centre applies a peer mentoring model to support tutees to develop academic skills that will help them succeed in their undergraduate courses.

This chapter is intended to fulfil three aims. Firstly, to shed light on the extent to which such an academic support centre may be used in the context of an EMI programme in Japan. That is, once a peer support service has become well-established in an EMI programme in Japan, how much ongoing demand is there for peer support?

Secondly, this chapter analyses feedback data collected at the centre over a period of one academic year to better understand the level of satisfaction of the users and what the students felt they learnt while using the centre. Feedback data was collected from both tutors and tutees over a period of one academic year in an attempt to evaluate the effectiveness of the support centre in fostering learning. The analysis of feedback data addresses two questions: How satisfied are tutors and tutees with the peer support sessions they are involved in? And, What do tutors and tutees believe they learn during peer tutorial sessions?

Finally, the chapter explores the relative effectiveness of peer support offered by tutors from different linguistic backgrounds. Tutees' satisfaction with sessions in which the tutor was from a traditional Japanese-medium educational background was compared with tutees' satisfaction with sessions in which the tutor was an international student from an Anglophone context to ascertain the relative effectiveness of the sessions offered by Japanese L1 and English L1 tutors. The purpose of this comparison is to find out, from the perspective of tutees, the relative effectiveness of Japanese domestic students and English L1 students employed as peer tutors in the Japanese EMI context.

Need for support services

Students who apply for admission to ETPs in Japan are typically required to meet certain English language proficiency benchmarks to be admitted. However, having met a specific English proficiency benchmark does not ensure that students will be capable of undertaking undergraduate classes in the medium of English. Students still need language and/or academic skills support (Bradford, 2013). Indeed, native English speaking students studying in the medium of English also often require academic skills support to bridge the gap between what they have learnt at high school and what is expected of them at the tertiary level. Such support has been offered on an increasingly large scale at universities throughout the world. One typical model is the North American "Writing Center" which has been in existence since the 1960s (Carino, 1995) and has been implemented at more and more universities in the United States as time goes by.

Another common form of academic support around the world is Peer Assisted Study Support (PASS). This form of support aims to help students to better understand the content of their classes and to perform better in assignments and tests. "They typically consist of sessions facilitated by PASS peer leaders who are current students who have successfully completed the course and have been trained to facilitate sessions with other students" (Leask, 2009, p. 208). PASS differs from the North American writing center model in that support is usually offered to groups of students. On the other hand, in writing centres, the most common organisation is one-to-one sessions between a peer tutor and a tutee. In both of these models, the use of a peer creates a casual atmosphere and this casual atmosphere breaks down barriers for some students allowing them to ask questions about the course content which they may not have the courage to ask the instructor or professional support staff.

One-to-one tutorial sessions between students offer some potential advantages over PASS group sessions. Firstly, a one-to-one context may be even less threatening than a peer group, especially for students who lack confidence. In this context, tutors can spend more time chatting casually and building rapport with their tutees which may encourage more willingness to share ideas on the part of less confident learners. Kelo (2006) states that Asian students, in particular, may be reluctant to ask questions and thus, peer support offered in a relaxed atmosphere may be especially important in the Asian context. Tutors can increase or decrease the amount of casual chatting according to the perceived needs of each individual tutee, creating an environment where tutees feel more confident in sharing ideas and asking even "stupid" questions. Not only the casual chatting, but the entire tutorial session can be tailored to the needs of the individual tutee.

On the other hand, Japan constitutes a collectivist culture, which emphasises group harmony over individuality (Carson & Nelson, 1994), suggesting that Japanese students may prefer to learn in group sessions with their peers than individually. McKinley (2011) conducted research on a writing centre within an ETP in Japan and found that introducing workshops in a group format dramatically increased usage of the writing centre. However, the research only looked at attendance at such workshops in the first semester that they were offered. It is unclear whether the attendance at workshops was able to be maintained over the long term. As stated by Thompson (2014), services are often initially well-received, but usage may decrease in time.

There are also difficulties inherent in peer support models. There is a certain contradiction in tutors seeing themselves as both peers and tutors at the same time (Trimbur, 1987). Although they are peers in one sense, peer tutors are usually more successful students (often employed based on their academic record). Furthermore, Harris (1992) suggests that when tutors are trained for the peer tutoring position, they stop being true peers and take on more of an educator role. This contradiction is incredibly difficult to resolve. Institutions put a great deal of time and effort into recruiting and training tutors in order to ensure that quality academic support is offered, yet in doing so, distance is placed between the tutor and tutee which has the potential to disrupt the casual, relaxed atmosphere aimed for.

Apart from bridging the gap between high school and university expectations, in the EMI context, there is often a cultural gap between the past and present educational context, which also creates a need for support services. Some international students in Kelo and Rogers' (2010) study stated that their academic skills were effective in their previous educational contexts, but that they needed support to transition to a new educational context which placed more emphasis on independent learning. However, the educational context in an internationalised university may not only be new to international students. In a non-Anglophone culture such as Japan, many international academic staff are employed to teach on EMI programmes and this may result in educational practices that are foreign to local students. Salem (2016, p. 160) found that the students who choose to visit the writing centre (in the North American context) are "those who were historically excluded from higher education" such as L2 students. In the EMI context, the situation is quite the contrary, instead of being excluded, or even on the periphery of the educational institution such students are in the majority, thus emphasising the importance of support services being available in such contexts.

Overall, both language and academic skills support should ideally be on offer in institutions offering ETPs in Japan. Despite students having reached a language proficiency benchmark prior to admission, this does not guarantee that their language proficiency is sufficient to cope with the demands of EMI. Also, while it may be useful to offer support for international students learning Japanese, the most important language focus of support services should be the language of instruction. In addition to language support, academic skills support is necessary to help students who have come from a different educational context to transition into a new one found in ETPs. Finally, the aims of the informal curriculum offered in the form of academic support services should be matched as closely as possible to those of the formal curriculum (Leask, 2009) in order to most effectively support students' progression through the formal curriculum.

Uptake of support

As reported in the previous chapter, out of the 19 or 20 undergraduate ETPs in Japan, at least three and as many as eight do not offer any student support services. Moreover, in many cases, the support offered does not go beyond writing support. However, apart from universities offering support, students need to take up support services if they are to be effective.

Numerous studies have investigated the usage of writing centres and academic support centres. Much of this research has been conducted in contexts where the local language is also the language of instruction. In 2003–2004 the Writing Center Research Project in the US found that writing centres there conducted anywhere between 30 and 5,624 tutorials per academic year (Griffin et al, 2010, as cited in Bromley, Northway & Schonberg, 2013), while in the same project two years later the number of tutorials ranged from 45 to 19,000. In their own study, Bromley, Northway and Schonberg (2013) found that at a large public university with 18,800 potential users, up to 1,000 tutorials were conducted per year, at a medium-sized university with 10,500 potential users, up to 3,000 tutorials were conducted each year and at a small university with 1,500 potential users, up to 900 tutorials were conducted per year. In both the large university and the small one, some students are required to make use of the writing centre, thus increasing usage rates. Salem (2016) surveyed students at the completion of their four-year degree programme and found that 22% of graduating students had used the writing centre at least once. Results of such studies do not necessarily generalise to EMI contexts where the majority of students are non-native speakers of the medium of instruction and where the majority of students share the same native language. Few studies have been conducted in the relatively new context of ETPs in Japan.

Focussing on students taking EMI courses who were not enrolled in ETPs, Ishikura (2015) found that Japanese students were less likely to recognise that they needed support, even when they recognised that they were struggling with their academic work. She goes on to suggest that this lack of recognition would lead to insufficient uptake of support service offerings. One of the students in her study demonstrated an attitude of needing to endure the hardships involved in EMI by herself. The conscientiousness of some Japanese students may lead them to feel that they are a burden to the university if they make use of support services and that they should work hard on their own to improve their academic performance. Another reason that students may be reluctant to visit an academic support centre is that they are often considered to be a remedial service (see North, 1984) and there may be stigma involved in going to a remedial service.

Ishikura (2015) observed gradual development through time of students taking EMI classes in terms of both language and academic skills. Some students in her study were unable to participate in class discussions when they joined EMI classes. However, through taking the same course several times, they became more capable of succeeding in the course and more engaged independent learners who could lead group discussions and support less capable and/or less engaged peers to participate. It is clear that the process of learning progresses at a different rate for each learner. Therefore, learners should not be limited to having to successfully complete a course the first time. On the other hand, the provision of support services, offered by these more capable and engaged learners may enable less capable and/or less engaged learners to achieve success without having to take a course multiple times and thus expedite the educational process.

Thompson (2014) and McKinley (2010) have conducted such studies in ETPs in Japan. Thompson (2014) stated that writing centres in Japan have struggled to attract users. In his context, there was a decline in usage from 66 individual tutorial sessions in the first half of 2012 to just 17 individual sessions in the second half. However, the author did not share information about the size of the programme. It is therefore difficult to compare Thompson's (2014) results with those of other studies such as Bromley, Northway and Schonberg (2013) and Salem (2016). McKinley (2010) surveyed just 15 students in an ETP with a writing centre and found that five had used the writing centre. The students had not yet graduated and it is possible that the number of users would increase with time until graduation. Theoretically, the ETP context means that there are a higher proportion of the kinds of students that could benefit from support: L2 students and students who are adjusting to a new educational context. Indeed, McKinley's (2010) study in Japan found higher usage rates than most of the studies in the North American context, despite surveying students during experience rather than at graduation.

Peer support

One of the five desirable educational practices identified by Kuh et al. (2010) was active/collaborative learning. In the process of expanding on what this means, Kuh et al. (2010) list several activities that could be considered to exemplify active/collaborative learning. Included in this list were: students teaching students, learning from peers and peer tutoring. Kuh et al. (2010) found that effective educational institutions validated the power of peers to help each other, including through peer tutoring and peer evaluation. This encouraged students to critically evaluate their own work and that of their peers. Arum and Roksa (2011) also mention that when two peers study together, they work in a self-directed way and there is the freedom to explore the topic of study. In this way, peer learning may be considered to be more student-centred than classroom learning.

Employing students as a means of support for their peers fosters the development of a positive learning community among students. Moust and Schmidt (1994a) found that students had more positive perceptions of peer tutors than staff tutors. In terms of internationalisation of education, Kelo (2006) found evidence that the involvement of international students in peer support programmes was considered to increase their success. She also found that students were more likely to pay attention to peers in this context than to a lecturer. More specifically, she found that students from Asian backgrounds tended to find it easier to ask questions to a peer than to a lecturer to a greater extent than students from other cultural backgrounds.

Apart from the more positive perceptions on the part of students, a great deal of research has found that peer support is as effective as or more effective than the support offered by professional support staff. Pascarella and Terenzini (2005) reviewed previous literature in the field of education. In general, they found that collaborative learning, in which students either study together or teach each other, led to increased achievement. Moust and Schmidt (1994b) also found that the employment of peer tutors and staff tutors did not lead to any difference in terms of tutees' mastery of course content. On the other hand, Oley (1992) randomly assigned students to receive tutoring from a faculty member or a peer and found that students who received peer tutoring performed better than those who received tutoring from a faculty member.

An additional benefit of support provided by peers over the more traditional model of support provided by support staff who are employed by the university is that there is an opportunity for twice the learning to take place, because not only does the receiver of support benefit, but the peer tutor or mentor benefits as well. In fact, previous research indicates that the provider of peer support usually benefits more than the receiver (Astin, 1993; Lansiquot & Rosalia, 2015;

Pascarella & Terenzini, 2005). Therefore, offering peer support may be overall more effective than professional support services as both the tutor and the tutee stand to enhance their academic achievement, whereas in the professional support model only the tutee's academic achievement is likely to be enhanced since the professional support staff are experts. In addition to reaping the academic benefits of tutoring, employing students also helps them in other ways, supporting their non-academic lives. Being able to successfully find employment may relieve both financial and psychological stress and if the employment is related to their academic studies, it is more likely to enhance rather than detract from their academic endeavours. Being employed as a peer supporter may increase academic achievement through the act of preparing for and conducting support sessions, which indirectly improves academic performance. In addition, earning money in this way makes it less likely for a student to seek non-academic employment, which may limit the amount of time they could spend on their studies.

The major advantage of peer support over professional support, which cannot be ignored, is cost. Clearly, students can be employed at a lower wage than professional staff, which can save an institution a great deal of money over the long term. Lee (1988) compared seven different kinds of student support services which were all intended to decrease dropout rates and increase retention. Although the study is somewhat dated now, services involving peers as resources were found to be effective at increasing retention rates and they were also shown to be very cost-effective, whereas traditional support services (usually offered by professional support staff) were found to be very cost-ineffective. On the other hand, it is also clear that to set up and maintain a system of peer support will require more organisational time than setting up a system of professional support. This is because a great deal of training and mentoring is required to prepare students for the role and to support them in the role. Student staff are also likely to be employed for shorter periods than professional staff. Thus, apart from more training being required, it will also be required more often if peer support is offered. As Kelo and Rogers (2010, p. 49) put it "while recognizing the benefits of student-to-student support, good practice seems to require that institutions take up the overarching responsibility for the accuracy, comprehensiveness, and quality of the services".

This chapter considers the extent to which there is likely to be ongoing demand for student support services within an ETP in Japan after the support services are well-established. With the hype around support services when they are first established, they have a tendency to be well utilised initially, with many students wanting to "try out" the new offering. However, as Thompson (2014) mentioned, such demand tends to recede once the service becomes established. This chapter will focus on the usage of a well-established centre in order to demonstrate the extent to which students may continue to utilise a service in the long-term. The research will focus specifically on peer support services, which may be less valued and therefore less demanded than professional support services in the Japanese context.

Evaluation of support services

Although student support services invariably have clear aims and objectives, measuring such aims and objectives is incredibly difficult. As succinctly stated by Topping (1996, p. 340):

> tutoring is usually a relatively small component of a relatively wide range of teaching and learning strategies deployed in higher education, so the extent to which it is realistic to expect associated gains to be measurable, widespread, maintained and generalized is debatable.

The purpose of this section is to provide a brief overview of the kinds of benefits of student support services that have been found in previous research.

It has been found in some studies (i.e. Topping, 1996; Williams & Takaku, 2011) that students who used support services performed better academically than those who did not. Williams and Takaku (2011) found that support services were particularly valuable for ESL students, who received the same support as domestic students and then outperformed the domestic students. Moreover, Banjong (2015) investigated the effectiveness of international students' use of a student success centre and found that more use of the student success centre significantly correlated with higher academic achievement.

One common underlying principle of student support services is that their use should be totally voluntary. This principle is held because the services fulfil a support role, helping students who want and/or need help to reach the primary objective of succeeding in their academic study. Those who want help will seek it voluntarily and there is, therefore, no necessity for institutions to intervene. Although various risk factors that predict academic difficulty have been found in previous research, there is no objective way of determining which individuals need support. Many universities have a system of reaching out to students who are less successful, and such systems are often based on the number of courses failed. Nevertheless, it is difficult to distinguish between those who are failing courses because of a lack of interest or effort and those who are making an effort but lack the language or academic skills necessary to succeed.

Because of the voluntary nature of student support services, accurate and objective measurement of the effectiveness of such services becomes difficult. Students come in with a wide range of motivations and competencies, making it difficult to determine how best to measure the effectiveness of the support they have received. Although extremely subjective, often the level of satisfaction on the part of users is the primary means of evaluating the effectiveness of such services. While the level of satisfaction cannot provide an objective measurement of effectiveness, it enables us to understand what is considered to be effective from the participants' perspective (Macauley, 2012).

This chapter will attempt to evaluate the effectiveness of a peer support service by evaluating the level of satisfaction of both tutors and tutees. Following this, the tutors' and tutees' perspectives of the learning that takes place during the peer support sessions will be examined. The arrangement of ongoing tutorial relationships facilitated the building of rapport between tutors and tutees and allowed for a maximally comfortable and friendly environment. On the other hand, this arrangement also complicated the process of evaluating levels of satisfaction, as each tutee and tutor are likely to have similar levels of satisfaction each time they participate in tutorial sessions with the same partner. Moreover, tutorial pairings that are felt to be more effective by tutees are likely to continue for longer than those that are felt to be less effective. Thus leading to an overrepresentation of the most effective sessions and underrepresentation of those that are less effective. Therefore, for data related to satisfaction with the support service, all tutorials for the same subject between the same tutor and tutee were combined and averaged so that each data line corresponds to one tutor-tutee relationship. This method leads to a more objective measurement of overall effectiveness as no tutorial pair is represented more in the data than any other. This is different from many previous studies (such as Bromley, Northway & Schonberg, 2013) which have included each feedback form as an individual case in the data.

Previous studies relating to writing centre assessment have noted a selection bias since students are busy and often leave without completing feedback questionnaires (e.g. Gofine, 2012; Bromley, Northway & Schonberg, 2013; Bromley, Northway & Schonberg, 2018). In the context of the present study, receiving feedback from users was considered important to the quality of the service and thus it was decided that the final five minutes of every one-hour session should be dedicated to the completion of feedback questionnaires.

Another significant difference between this study and previous studies is that feedback questionnaires are often completed only by tutees. In centres where professional support staff are employed, there is no doubt that this practice is appropriate. However, in the context of peer support services, it would seem valuable to ask both tutors and tutees to complete questionnaires as both tutors and tutees are enrolled students in the institution and both are likely to enhance their academic performance through their participation in tutorials. Indeed, it would seem that an evaluation of a peer support service which only asked tutees to complete questionnaires would only be evaluating half of the potential learning and development that was occurring in the centre.

Linguistic background of tutors

A greater amount of research has been conducted in relation to the linguistic background of teachers than of peer tutors. Since teachers and peer tutors are two different educator roles, both kinds of research will be discussed here. Lasagabaster and Sierra (2002) asked students about their preference for native or non-native English speaking teachers at a range of different educational levels. The students reported preferring native English speaking teachers, or a combination of native and non-native English speaking teachers over non-native English speaking teachers alone. The students' experiences of having been taught by teachers from different linguistic backgrounds did not seem to have any effect on this preference. On the other hand, Wilkinshaw and Duong (2012) found that other factors were more important to students than whether or not a teacher was a native speaker of English. Students in their study seemed to consider native-speaker status as an unimportant factor.

Teachers are supposed to be experts in the subject they teach. On the other hand, peer tutors are not expected to be experts; they are supposed to be supportive peers who understand the struggles of other students and can help them by sharing their own experiences. When we consider these respective roles, it would seem that native-speaker status should be much less of an issue in the context of peer tutoring. Yet writing centres are one of the main contexts in which peer tutors are employed and research on writing centres has largely ignored non-native English speaking tutors (Zhao, 2017). While there has been a great deal of research on the tutoring of non-native English speaking students in the writing centre, it is often assumed that all tutors are native speakers of English and thus their linguistic background is not even mentioned (Zhao, 2017). Therefore, there is very little evidence of the relative effectiveness of native speaking and non-native speaking tutors in relation to one-to-one tutorial support.

LeClare and Franz (2013) state that the absence of peer tutors is one of the distinguishing features of writing centres in an EFL environment. The same could be said of those in EMI environments in non-Anglophone countries. As has been demonstrated in chapter two, peer tutors are rarely employed in the Japanese context. LeClare and Franz (2013) state their assumption that the employment of non-native English speaking tutors would increase the use of the centre by non-native English speaking tutees and suggest that the absence of non-native English speaking tutors in their context resulted in limited use of the centre by undergraduate students. In addition to the potential to discourage students from using the centre, employing exclusively international students as tutors may make it difficult to attract enough tutors. A study by Thompson (2014), was conducted in a writing centre in an ETP in Japan which employed international exchange students as peer tutors. However, the centre faced administrative challenges, notably a small number of international exchange students limited the pool of potential tutors who could be employed in the centre.

Zhao (2017) conducted a study in which one tutee participated in writing centre sessions with one native English speaking and one non-native English speaking tutor. The student demonstrated a preference for the native English speaking tutor. However, the author suggested that the stated preference for a native English speaking tutor may have been for a tutor that directly corrected the student's linguistic errors, which in this case the native English speaking tutor did, while the non-native English speaking tutor did not. This is similar to the finding of McKinley (2011). In his study, most tutors were native English speaking tutors. However, tutees who used the centre expressed an expectation that their papers would be edited for linguistic accuracy by the tutors and were not satisfied with the sessions when this did not occur. Okuda (2019) focussed on a writing centre in Japan where four Japanese students received tutoring sessions from Japanese tutors. Okuda suggests that non-native English-speaking tutors should not only be employed to conduct tutorial sessions in the local language, but also provide tutoring sessions to a diverse range of students in English as they serve as effective role models.

A more systematic analysis of native English speaking and non-native English speaking tutors was conducted by Park and Shin (2010), with four tutors (two from each linguistic background) and four tutees (all non-native English speakers) making up four tutorial pairs (two non-native English speaking pairs and two mixed pairs). Each pair participated in three one-to-one writing tutorials. In Park and Shin's (2010) study, the students found that the possibility of code-switching in the non-native English speaking pair sessions facilitated the negotiation of meaning and resulted in a more satisfactory tutorial experience. Overall, Park and Shin (2010) recommended a balance of native English speaking and non-native English speaking tutors to be employed in writing centres.

In the non-Anglophone context, being a non-native English speaker is an important part of what it means to be a peer. Murphey (1998) argues that Near Peer Role Models (successful language usersfrom the same culture, at a similar age) can significantly affect students' motivation and strategy choice. The final purpose of the research reported in this chapter was to determine whether the linguistic background of peer tutors had any significant impact on the effectiveness of the one-to-one tutorial sessions they offered.

The Academic Support Centre

The centre under investigation in this chapter is an Academic Support Centre, located within a self-access centre in an undergraduate ETP in Japan. To be eligible to become a tutor, a cumulative Grade Point Average (GPA) of 3.0 or higher was required (a B average). In order to tutor language proficiency tests, tutors were required to have taken the relevant test within the last three years and to have received over 550 in TOEFL ITP, over 80 in TOEFL iBT and 6.5 in IELTS. These eligibility requirements were not considered very high. The average cumulative GPA across the university was 3.05 as at the end of the 2016 academic year and the average TOEFL ITP score of incoming first-year students is around 520 to 540 each semester. Thus, even students with average academic achievement could become tutors if they were motivated to do so.

Once the successful applicants had been selected, they were required to successfully complete tutor training before they were officially employed and began tutoring in the centre. Tutor training entailed participation in a six-hour tutor training workshop, observing a one-hour long peer tutorial session and writing an observation report, conducting a one-hour long peer tutorial session while being observed by an incumbent tutor, who wrote an observation report and finally a post-training interview with the coordinator, who read both observation reports and interviewed the applicant in order to ensure that they had grasped the important tenets of the tutor training process. Once the interview had been successfully completed, tutors were officially employed and started working in the centre. If it was considered that the applicant had not grasped the important tenets of the training, further observed sessions were conducted, with support from the incumbent peer tutor observer, until the tutor was considered competent.

The support was offered in the form of one-hour long one-to-one peer tutorial sessions. Sessions were offered in a range of subjects as follows:

- Academic writing
- Academic reading
- Academic presentations
- TOEFL ITP Reading
- TOEFL ITP Written expression
- TOEFL iBT Reading
- TOEFL iBT Writing
- IELTS Reading
- IELTS Writing
- Maths for liberal arts
- College Algebra
- Statistics
- Calculus
- Biology
- Japanese language

The support offered by the centre was marketed to both faculty and students. However, the amount of marketing was not a great deal due to the lack of time and budget. The centre coordinator was also a full-time instructor at the university, resulting in limited time availability and students were paid by the hour for their work for the centre, resulting in budgetary constraints. The coordinator and a few peer tutors gave a presentation in the orientation course that all first-year students were required to pass in the first semester of their studies. The presentation covered an introduction of the services offered by the centre and an introduction to the online reservation system. A similar presentation was also given during the orientation week for incoming international exchange students in the week before their classes began. The session for international exchange students included the introduction to the services offered by the centre and the online reservation system as well as discussion of academic plagiarism and how to become a tutor in the centre.

Apart from the orientation sessions for incoming students, each class for which tutorial support was considered to be helpful received a visit from a peer tutor briefly at some stage during each semester. During the visit, the tutor introduced the support and the online reservation system and explained in a personal manner how the tutorial support might help for the particular course the students were taking. The tutor who visited each class tutored in the subject relevant to the class and had taken the class before themselves, enabling them to take a more tailored approach to the visit. It was hoped that seeing a peer tutor's face would make the peer support service seem more approachable to potential users.

In principle, students could request up to two tutorial sessions per week, with each one-hour tutorial session being dedicated to just one subject. Therefore, at a maximum, a tutee could receive tutorial support in two different subjects within one week. These limits were implemented due to budgetary restrictions which precluded the centre from allowing students to receive unlimited support. No drop-in services were offered at the centre. This meant that the only time peer tutors were paid for was the time spent marketing the centre and tutoring. Bookings were made through the online booking system and a tutor received their tutoring schedule in advance, only going to the centre when sessions had been booked. This enabled the centre to offer more sessions on a smaller budget as tutors were never paid for sitting in the centre unused.

In the centre under investigation, the default arrangement was for the tutee to have ongoing weekly sessions with the same tutor for the same subject. This was relatively frequently increased to twice-weekly sessions or decreased to fortnightly sessions in order to allow a student to receive support in just one subject or more than two subjects overall. If a tutee wanted to change to a different tutor, they could stop these sessions at any time and make a new request through the online booking system to be matched with a new tutor.

The curriculum at the university is somewhat flexible. Although there are a number of courses that need to be passed for graduation, it is not required to take all courses at the same year level at the same time. This means that in some cases, first-year students and fourth-year students take the same course at the same time. This flexibility in the curriculum has the effect of somewhat reducing the importance of seniority amongst students compared to some other universities in Japan. For this reason, whether the tutor offering a session was older than a tutee participating in a session varied. In this centre, age was not emphasised and it was considered that anyone who had taken the relevant course and received the required grade was capable of tutoring anyone else in the subject, regardless of age or length of academic experience.

Some centre history

In the academic support centre in focus in this chapter, there have been some historical policy changes that should be described in order to better understand the context. Japanese-language background tutors have always been employed as peer tutors at the centre and English-language background tutors started to be employed not long after the centre was established in April 2010. The number of English-language background tutors has gradually increased in line with the increasing number of English-language background students at the university. No attempt has ever been made to influence the number of tutors with different language backgrounds who become tutors; the best applicants are always selected on the basis of the current needs of the centre.

The language policy of the centre was to assume that sessions were to be conducted in English. Tutors were instructed to greet the tutee in English and begin the session, assuming that it would be conducted in English. However, if the tutee requested for the tutor to speak in Japanese, it was fine for them to do so and if the tutee code-switched, it was fine for the tutor to also code-switch in the same way. Overall, as long as the tutor was capable of speaking Japanese, the language used during tutorial sessions was determined by the tutee rather than the tutor.

Initially, students could specify who they would like to have a tutorial with and they would be matched with the tutor they selected when the session was scheduled. However, in time, it was found that the sign-up process resulted in a popularity contest, the result being that the tutors with the widest circle of friends and acquaintances would receive significantly more requests, and consequently, significantly more income. In time, this was considered unfair as other tutors were equally qualified and trained for the position but could not earn as much money from the position due to having entered the university more recently or even being more shy. Thus, the system was changed so that tutees could not specify which tutor they wanted to receive tutorials from. The coordinator in charge of scheduling would ignore such requests if they were made and match any tutee with any tutor on the basis of the tutee's and tutor's availability and would attempt to offer the same number of tutorial sessions to each tutor. This study was conducted after this policy change, at a time when tutees could not request a specific tutor. It remains unclear the extent to which the language background of a tutor is likely to have a significant effect on tutee satisfaction with tutorial sessions.

Data and analysis

Centre usage

Demand for the support service will be investigated by considering the usage rates of the centre over the 2016 academic year (April 2016 to February 2017). The centre had been in operation for six years by this time and it was considered that usage rates in the seventh year of operation should be sustainable over the long term.

Satisfaction and reported learning

From the fall semester of 2015 until the end of the 2016 academic year, both tutors and tutees were required to provide feedback at the end of each session. The feedback questionnaires were developed collaboratively between the centre coordinator and a small group of peer tutors. This chapter will analyse the data from one year – The 2016 academic year. The questionnaires elicited feedback both about the level of satisfaction of both the tutor and the tutee with each session and their perceptions of what they learnt through the session. The feedback questionnaire completed by tutors can be seen in Appendix B and that of tutees can be seen in Appendix C.

Satisfaction levels of tutors and tutees were analysed by numerically coding the results and then calculating the average scores of both the tutor and the tutee within each individual tutor-tutee relationship. The tutors' and tutees' perspectives of the learning that occurred during the sessions will be summarised through coding and grouping the qualitative responses to the open-ended questionnaire questions.

Linguistic background of tutors

To analyse tutee's relative satisfaction with tutorial sessions offered by tutors from different linguistic backgrounds, the tutee satisfaction and reported learning data were grouped in relation to the linguistic background of the tutor conducting the session. There were three groups: traditional Japanese educational background students who had been educated in the Japanese school system until the end of secondary school, bilingual background students who had mixed heritage, had spent time living abroad, or who had attending international schools prior to entering university, and English background students who did not have any Japanese heritage and had studied in an English-medium context until the end of secondary school. This study focussed on tutors from the first and third groups; Japanese background students and native English speaking students. These two groups are specific groups of students who are clearly defined. The second group was a very diverse group, consisting of students from a wide range of backgrounds. It was felt that including the second group would not provide any useful information because of the diversity within the group.

In order to make a clear comparison between the effectiveness of Japanese background tutors and native-English background tutors to support EMI students, three types of data were excluded from this study. Feedback data relating to tutorial sessions for Japanese language support were not included in this analysis. The data from the tutorial sessions offered by bilingual students were also discarded for this analysis. Some participants had not provided sufficient information about their background to determine which group they belonged to. The data relating to the sessions conducted by those tutors were also discarded.

The definition of bilingual students in this study was extremely broad in order to be very clear about the specific background of the Japanese speaking students and native English speaking students. A large number of students enter the university to a greater or lesser extent bilingual, so excluding the second group of students reduced the amount of data significantly (this reduced the amount of data by more than half, as more than half of the sessions were offered by bilingual background students). Out of the tutorial sessions for which both tutor and tutee feedback data were available, 344 were offered by Japanese background tutors and 208 were offered by native English speaking tutors. Therefore, feedback data on these 552 sessions were analysed in this study.

Independent samples t-tests were conducted between the satisfaction data of the sessions conducted by traditional Japanese background students and those conducted by the native English speaking students in order to determine whether there was any statistically significant difference in satisfaction between the sessions conducted by the students from these two linguistic backgrounds. Qualitative responses to the feedback form were also analysed and compared between groups. The results of this analysis and some example comments will be offered to illustrate the feelings of tutees towards sessions offered by tutors from different linguistic backgrounds.

Usage of the centre

The ETP consists of approximately 800 undergraduate students at any time. Of those 800, approximately 600 are on campus and the remaining approximately 200 are studying abroad. The study abroad is conducted on the basis of a reciprocal exchange whereby one Japanese student studies abroad at a host institution for a period of one year and in return the institution abroad sends either one student for a period of one year or two students for a period of one semester each to study in Japan. This means that at any time, there are also approximately 200 short-term international exchange students on campus. Of these 800 students on campus, approximately 30 are employed in the centre as peer tutors in any semester. Since the students who work as tutors in the centre are likely to see the benefits of peer tutorial sessions, including peer tutors who also use the centre as tutees may bias usage rates. Therefore, peer tutors were excluded from usage rates, even when they used the centre as a tutee, leaving approximately 770 undergraduate students as potential users of the peer tutorial service.

In the 2016 academic year, 2006 peer tutorial sessions were conducted by 34 peer tutors. These included 847 (42%) sessions for academic skills support, 466 (23%) sessions for language proficiency test support, 401 (20%) sessions for maths/science support and 294 (15%) sessions for Japanese language support. On average, each peer tutor conducted around 60 sessions over the 30 weeks of the semester (two sessions per week). These 2006 sessions were conducted with 156 individual tutees. Therefore, each tutee participated in 13 sessions, on average, over the 30-week academic year (just less than one session every two weeks). Furthermore, approximately one in five students who were not tutors used the tutorial service during the academic year in question (20%).

Student satisfaction

The 34 tutors and 156 tutees included in this analysis participated in the 2006 tutorial sessions in 515 individual pairs. That is; each pair met for four sessions, on average, over the one-year period. On average, each tutee met with three different tutors throughout the academic year and each tutor met with 15 different tutees. The satisfaction data will be averaged by tutorial pair in order to prevent tutorial pairs who met more often from being overrepresented in the data, thus likely inflating the reported satisfaction levels.

Table 3.1 shows the reported learning during sessions and Table 3.2 shows satisfaction with sessions on the part of tutors. The descriptive statistics show that learning about the tutee was the most frequently reported learning on the part of tutors, followed by learning about the subject they were tutoring. In just over one-third of the sessions, tutors reported learning something about tutoring.

Table 3.1 Reported learning of tutors

Question	Mean	SD	Minimum	Maximum
Q1. Learning about the tutee	63%	42%	0%	100%
Q2. Learning about tutoring	34%	43%	0%	100%
Q3. Learning about the subject	38%	44%	0%	100%

$n = 515$

Table 3.2 Satisfaction of tutors

Question	Mean	SD	Minimum	Maximum
Q4. Satisfaction	3.56	0.50	2	4

$n = 515$

Table 3.3 shows the satisfaction of tutees in relation to whether the tutor understood their needs, level of confidence in the subject and satisfaction with the sessions. Table 3.4 shows the frequency with which they learnt something during a session. The descriptive statistics demonstrate that tutees feel that they learn something new about the subject they receive support in more than 97% of the time.

A paired samples t-test was conducted between the satisfaction levels of tutors and tutees and it was found that tutees were significantly

Table 3.3 Satisfaction of tutees

Question	Mean	SD	Minimum	Maximum
Q1. Tutor understanding of your needs	3.73	0.37	2	4
Q3. Confidence in the subject	3.23	0.59	1	4
Q4. Satisfaction	3.77	0.40	2	4

$n = 515$

Table 3.4 Reported learning of tutees

Question	Mean	SD	Minimum	Maximum
Q2. Learning about the subject	97%	13%	0%	100%

$n = 515$

more satisfied with the sessions than the tutors were: t (514) = 7.592, $p = <0.001$.

Out of the 515 tutorial pairs analysed, there were 83 in which the tutor reported not having learnt anything (16%). However, the tutors received payment for their sessions and obtained experience as a peer tutor. Therefore, although learning something during a session is beneficial, it is not a necessary component of the tutor experience. On the other hand, there were no tutorial pairs in which the tutee reported not having learnt anything. In every tutorial pair, the tutee learnt something at least 70% of the time (one pair), there was one tutorial pair in which the tutee reported learning something 80% of the time and there were a further two tutorial pairs in which the tutee learnt something 90% of the time. In the remaining 99.2% of tutorial pairs (511) learning occurred for the tutee in every session.

Qualitative reports of learning

In analysing the answers to the open-ended questions, it became clear that there was a wide range of aspects of learning mentioned by both tutees and tutors. This section will examine the responses to the open-ended questions separately for each subject area tutored. The responses were analysed and grouped into categories thematically, with the categories emerging from the data. The data was recoded three times until felicity was found between the coding of each comment.

Academic skills support

The responses of tutors relating to peer tutorial sessions for academic skills support fell into four groups: 234 comments related to tutors learning about tutoring (229) or increasing their understanding of the curriculum at the university (5), 127 comments related to learning about qualities or characteristics of the tutee (79) or learning strategies or approaches employed by the tutee (48) and 115 comments related to learning something about the academic skill area in focus.

Tutors experienced a wide range of learning about tutoring. For example, one tutor commented that "Some people mistake a research question for a thesis statement", while another commented that "It is important to make sure a tutee knows what their research question is and that they are answering it fully." One tutor commented that "Writing down what the tutee said on the whiteboard helps the tutee to cognitively understand their own thoughts.", while another commented that "Asking questions and encouraging the tutee to speak and write down their ideas helps with the tutee's thought process." A different tutor found that "Going through both the text and the rubric helped the tutee to ease her anxiety for the assignment." Another found that "Some people just need reassurance and a lot less technical assistance."

Regarding their learning about the curriculum at the university, tutors offered comments such as "Seeing the different types of essays he has brought in this semester, I understand the EAP course a bit better and will probably be able to help future students a bit better.", and "Professor A's students lack the knowledge of the basic structure of a research paper."

The qualities or characteristics of learners that tutors pointed out included being well organised (this comment was made 16 times), attentive and/or passive (10 times), good at correcting their own writing (9 times), active and/or ask a lot of questions (9 times) and a quick learner (this comment was made 8 times). Comments about the learning strategies or approaches employed by tutees included that the tutee reads and/or writes multilingually (4 times), "learns through examples" (3 times), is a visual learner (2 times), and a collaborative learner (2 times).

Regarding what the tutors learnt about academic skills, they mentioned that "It's hard to balance opinion and synthesis of ideas.", that "It is difficult to write an objective synthesis of ideas.", while another noted that "Being specific and certain is necessary for essay writing."

The learning reported by the tutees was more closely related to the subject on which the session was focussed. One hundred and eighty-five comments expressed learning about how to organise ideas within writing, 90 comments conveyed learning related to logical explanation, providing sufficient support for or development of ideas, 68 expressed learning about grammar, 54 reported learning about new resources or strategies that they could use in their self-directed study, and comments about appropriate academic style and vocabulary use were made 45 times each.

The comments relating to the organisation of ideas included "How to find the relationship between each paragraph.", and "How to make my topic sentences clearer." That the comments related to the organisation of ideas were more than twice as frequent as comments about any other aspects of writing suggests that this was the predominant focus of tutorial sessions for academic skills.

Comments relating to logical explanation, providing sufficient support for or development of ideas included the following: "I could get a new perspective of my research topic.", "How I should support my essays and what sources I need to do so.", "How to elaborate the ideas in each argument paragraph." and "To check if my entire essay is logically coherent is important." This was the second-largest group of comments suggesting a relatively frequent focus on these kinds of issues during the academic skills sessions.

Comments about grammar included statements such as: "I learned when to put commas in my writing.", I learned the difference between a semi-colon and a colon." and "I learned how to make various clauses in a sentence." There were also some less specific comments, in which students simply reported learning about grammar.

Slightly less frequently than comments related to grammar, there were comments which pinpointed learning about new resources or strategies that they could use in their self-directed study. These comments included "How to do brainstorming.", "How to find effective references and create an outline." and "My tutor taught me about useful internet dictionary sites to search for synonyms and proper words for my essay."

The comments relating to academic style included "Using more than three successive words can be calculated as plagiarism.", "How to correctly use APA citation style, including author's name and publication year." and "How to write my introduction and conclusion more softly." Those relating to vocabulary use included "I learnt how significant word choice is.", "The word 'human' is impersonal, so I should use 'people' instead."

Language proficiency test support

The responses of tutors relating to peer tutorial sessions for proficiency test support fell into three groups: 174 comments related to learning about qualities or characteristics of the tutee, 165 comments related to learning about tutoring, 35 comments related to learning about the proficiency test or the scoring of the test and 11 comments related to learning strategies or approaches employed by the tutee.

The comments relating to learning about qualities or characteristics of the learner included such comments as "This tutee is great at answering questions pertaining to details but struggles more in questions which have implied answers.", "She often thinks too much about the topic of the reading and will come to her own conclusion about what the answer should be.", and "She is always great about asking questions. If she doesn't understand fully or is still a bit confused even after my answer, she will continue to ask until she is satisfied."

The comments relating to learning about tutoring included: "I relearned that since I am merely supporting the tutee, it is effective to keep asking the tutee what types of strategies she used and its pros and cons.", "Concentration span and pace is different for every tutee. Some tutees need more time than others.", and "There is a huge difference between scaffolding and telling them the answers. In order to make them feel better the former is really important."

Although a small number of comments related to learning about the proficiency test or the scoring of the test, there were some such comments. For example, "Building a strong pool of vocabulary is essential in scoring around the 55 range.", "Skimming is a critical technique.", "The TOEFL ITP test is outdated and uses grammatical structures that are not really necessary." were comments made by tutors.

The tutees' comments related to their learning during language proficiency test support tutorial sessions included: 14 comments which reported learning about the (requirements of the) test they were preparing to take, eight comments relating to methods or strategies for preparing for or using during the proficiency test, five comments which mentioned learning about features of the English language, and two comments which related to a change in their mindset towards the test they were preparing to take. The number of comments made by tutees which reported learning was small as many of the comments simply reported what was covered during the session without mentioning specific takeaways.

The 14 comments relating to learning about the test included comments about the test itself such as "I did not know that grammar is counted for 25% of the essay score." and "My essay will be evaluated with 3 or 4 criteria; vocabulary, grammar, organization and ideas." and comments about the requirements of the test tasks such as "I understood that I should write a conclusion at the end of each paragraph." and "I should state a thesis first. Also, the structure is more important than originality."

The eight comments relating to methods or strategies included commenting on methods or strategies for preparing for the test, such as "I learnt that extensive reading is really important." and "I found some good online resources to support my study." As well as methods or strategies to be used while taking the test, such as "If I can't understand some words, it's important to skip them." and "[In the reading section] I should focus on the first paragraph most".

The five comments relating to language each explained specific points about the English language that the tutee learnt during the session, such as "'People' can be used as a verb (but very infrequently)", "After 'much' the noun must be in singular form" and "-ty at the end of a word means noun. For example, severity is the noun [form] of severe."

The last group of comments consisted of only two comments: "Before I came to the [centre], I felt so nervous about taking IELTS exam. However, the tutor told me some tips and encouraged me. So I have more confidence and think I can do better than before." and "I became more motivated." Despite only consisting of two comments, this category was seen as important to include in the analysis because affective factors play an important part in test-taking.

Mathematics and science support

The comments made by tutors of maths and science sessions included 74 comments relating to the qualities of the tutee, 56 comments relating to learning more about tutoring or about the curriculum at the university and 33 comments which expressed further learning about mathematics and science, or methods or strategies for learning mathematics or for solving mathematical problems.

The 74 comments relating to learning about qualities of the tutee involved in the session, included such comments as "For this tutee it seemed that even if she understands the concepts, she finds it difficult to solve the problems", "[This tutee] is very argumentative. She does not take my explanations the way they are, she tries to rephrase them so that she can understand them well, which I think is really good.", and "She came to the [centre] to ask a few last-minute questions [before the final exam]. However, some of the questions were about the basics, so I am afraid that she does not understand the overall concepts. I wish she would have studied about the basics before going on to calculations so that she could understand statistics as a whole."

The 56 comments relating to increased understanding of tutoring or of the curriculum at the university included the following comments: "Even though I understand how to solve the problems by myself in my head it is still difficult to explain the solutions to a person in a way that that person will understand.", "Letting the tutee explain about what he understood is very helpful to see if the tutee really understood.", "Statistics has more English involved than other maths subjects, so it is difficult to balance the amount of Japanese I use in the session. The tutee wanted to know the terms in Japanese, so I told him the words in Japanese once, but I tried to use English vocabulary since the class will use the English terms."

The 33 comments relating to further learning about maths and science, included insights such as "I learnt how Americans calculate", "I learnt well about one to one correspondence, which I was not sure of before. I thought explaining about the concept to the tutee helped me to understand more about it.", and "Since I teach the solutions to the same problems to many tutees, I see the same problems repeatedly. I think this helps me to understand the subject better."

The learning that the tutees reported in their comments could be simply categorised into two groups: 66 comments related to learning specific subject matter in the area of mathematics or science (58) or English terminology, the language required to understand the mathematics and science in English (8), the remaining 12 comments related to affective factors.

The learning of specific maths and science subject matter was conveyed in comments such as "How to utilize Excel for calculations.", "I had never heard the learning example about inverse function. This example made inverse function understandable for me.", and "I reviewed the contents covered in my class so I should have learned nothing new, but I realized many new things that I had been missing/misunderstanding.".

The eight comments relating to English terminology required to understand maths and science in English included: "I learnt the difference between mutually exclusive and independent.", "I learned how to distinguish 'permutation' from '*kumiawase*'.", and "I learned what 'cardinally' means." These comments show the importance of understanding the terminology of a discipline in order to be able to achieve subject learning within that discipline.

The final group of comments about learning made by maths and science tutees related to affective factors. These comments included: "This tutor taught me statistics clearly and kindly. His sessions motivated me to study statistics more and I have gradually become confident in the subject." and "The way of tutoring always makes me understand the exercises for this subject on my own, which is very motivating. He goes straight to the points that I do not understand and the speed of learning is perfect for me. We covered a lot.".

Japanese language support

The tutors who support the Japanese language in the centre are all Japanese Language Education students in the graduate degree programme. Perhaps, for this reason, the majority of the comments which reported learning on the part of the Japanese language tutors were related to learning about tutoring, or about teaching Japanese (109). The second-largest group of comments (66) related to learning about qualities of the tutee involved in the session, or particular methods or strategies that are effective for the tutee. The third group (38) related to learning about the Japanese language (34), or about the subject matter that the learner's assignment focussed on (4).

The comments relating to learning about tutoring or teaching included: "Every tutee has their own learning style and speed, so we should observe them well.", "I change tutoring style for each tutee, maybe based on my assumption about the tutee and their learning style. But if I want to foster learner autonomy in the tutees I should lead them to control the session when I can.", "One time there was an awkward silence because I waited too long. Then I explained that tutors are not teachers so we try not to teach. Then she started talking more, so that worked." and "When I do sessions with him I act differently from the way I act with other tutees. Since he comes with his own problems and questions, I act more like a language resource than a facilitator of learning. I think it is an interesting feature of being a native-speaking tutor."

Comments relating to learning about qualities of the tutee, included "It is necessary to repeat the same item that we have learned before. If he does not have any chance to use the item, he forgets it soon.", "He is linguistically aware. He notices a lot of details in sentence structures that other tutees don't." and "She is a very curious learner. She asked me some questions about small differences in nuances that other learners may not wonder about."

The comments relating to tutors' learning about the Japanese language included: "I learned how we organize a presentation in Japanese.", "I personally learned how the passive form was used in Japanese." and "I realized that modern conversation is very different from formal speech in Japanese. It is very important to understand the context when we speak Japanese.". Comments relating to tutors' learning about a subject matter not directly related to the Japanese language included: "Even though I feel that something is common in Japanese society, it is not necessarily common in other cultures.", "There are so many Jpop groups in Japan, but some of them are more popular internationally than in Japan." and "I learned some proverbs that have the same meaning in Korean and

Japanese but use different expressions." These comments demonstrate an increase in intercultural understanding on the part of tutors of the Japanese language. Tutorials in this group are cross-cultural by nature because almost all of the students who tutor the Japanese language are Japanese nationals, whereas almost all tutees who receive Japanese language support are non-Japanese.

Similarly to tutees who participated in Language Proficiency Test support sessions, the number of comments made by tutees in Japanese language support sessions which reported learning was small as many of the comments simply reported what was covered during the session without mentioning specific takeaways. Of the few comments that did report specific learning, 11 mentioned specific aspects of the language that they had learnt, two mentioned learning related to Japanese culture, one commented on learning a useful method of studying Japanese and two mentioned increased confidence.

The 11 comments mentioning specific aspects of the Japanese language that were learnt included: "I learnt the differences between causative sentences, causative passive sentences and passive sentences.", "I learnt the difference between the nuance of several terms, such as *'mou sugu'* versus *'sugu'; 'moshi...nara'* versus *'moshi...nattemo'*, and when to use *'takusan + no'* and when to use *takusan'* alone." and "I realized that I make fewer grammatical errors in my writing since coming to the [centre]. Also, I am able to communicate my questions to my tutor in Japanese now and she answers them effectively." The comments that focussed on learning related to Japanese culture included one tutee who reported learning about holidays in Japan and another who reported learning "about cultural differences between Korea and Japan".

Overall dimensions of learning

Dimensions of learning that received more than 10 comments overall from tutors, included increased learning about tutoring (with 558 comments overall), personal qualities of the tutees as learners (391), increased learning about the subject matter in focus (214), learning about strategies or methods that are effective for the tutee (64) and increased understanding about the curriculum at the university (10). Without exception, this reported learning will help the tutors to further develop their tutoring skills, offering more and more effective peer support sessions.

Dimensions of learning that were commented on more than 10 times by tutees included learning about the subject in focus (with 331 comments), learning strategies or methods for further self-study (63), affective factors (most commonly increased confidence or decreased anxiety in the subject in focus) (16) and learning specific features of the English language (13). The learning reported by tutees is likely to help them to achieve increased academic success in the English medium environment.

Satisfaction and reported learning by linguistic background

Descriptive statistics for the satisfaction data of the students who took part in tutorial sessions with Japanese background and English L1 tutors can be seen in Table 3.5 and reported learning can be seen in Table 3.6.

As can be seen from the descriptive statistics, the tutees reported a higher level of satisfaction with the tutorial sessions offered by Japanese language background tutors than with those offered by English language background tutors, with the mean result of every question being higher for the sessions offered by Japanese language background tutors. Independent samples t-tests were employed with a Bonferroni adjustment to determine whether these differences were statistically significant. It was found that in terms of the tutors understanding the tutees' needs, tutees' learning about the subject and the tutees' confidence in the subject, there was no significant difference between groups (Q1: $t(368.377) = 1.323$, $p = .187$, Q2: $t(550) = 0.421$, $p = .674$, Q3: $t(426.736) = 2.287$, $p = .023$). On the other hand, the difference between the tutees' overall satisfaction with the tutorial sessions offered by Japanese language background tutors

Table 3.5 Satisfaction of tutees by tutor linguistic background

Question	Japanese speaking tutors Mean (SD)	English speaking tutors Mean (SD)
Q1. Tutor understanding of your needs	3.78 (0.35)	3.74 (0.43)
Q3. Confidence in the subject	3.28 (0.69)	3.14 (0.71)
Q4. Satisfaction	3.87 (0.35)	3.68 (0.51)

Table 3.6 Reported learning of tutees by tutor linguistic background

Question	Japanese speaking tutors Mean (SD)	English speaking tutors Mean (SD)
Q2. Learning about the subject	99 % (12%)	98 % (14%)

and English language background tutors was statistically significant; $t(326.958) = 4.608$, $p = <.001$. This result indicates that overall tutees were significantly more satisfied with tutorial sessions offered by Japanese background tutors than with those offered by English background tutors. It is hoped that the analysis of qualitative data collected through open-ended feedback questions will shed light on reasons for this difference.

Appendix C provides the questions that were used to collect the qualitative data analysed here. The first question asked tutees to describe what they had learnt during the session. The second question asked "What went well or not so well during this session?" The first comment box yielded comments from 41% of tutees who participated in sessions with English language background tutors and 52% of tutees who participated in sessions with Japanese language background tutors. The second question yielded comments from 19% of tutees who participated in sessions with English language background tutors and 47% of tutees who participated in sessions with Japanese language background tutors. Therefore, the first result of this analysis is that tutees who participated in sessions with Japanese background tutors were more likely to offer comments.

Description of learning

The data were classified into two themes, coded and instances of each code counted. The classifications emerging from these comments were: a skill, strategy or how to do something, and a concept, fact, or idea that was learnt.

Describing a skill, strategy or how to do something was the most frequent type of comment by students in both groups. This kind of learning was described by 24% of tutees participating in sessions with English language background tutors and 23% of tutees participating in sessions with Japanese language background tutors. Examples of such comments follow:

English language background tutors.

- I learnt the way to skim the academic reading – going through introduction, conclusion, headlines, and the first and last sentence of each paragraph and chapter.
- How to use a hypothesis and key points in my writing.
- She showed me some very useful websites such as synonym dictionary and tips for academic writing.

Japanese language background tutors.

- Learnt how to draw a map to have a better understanding.

- I learnt how to spot and correct certain weird grammatical expressions in my writing.
- I learnt some common mistakes that I make when writing sentences. In particular, I learnt how to watch out for the subject of sentences and how the subject influences the verbs that I choose.

Describing a concept, fact or idea that was learnt was the less frequent type of comment by students in both groups. This kind of learning was described by 4% of tutees participating in sessions with English language background tutors and 5% of tutees participating in sessions with Japanese language background tutors. Examples of such comments follow:

English language background tutors.

- The way of reading depends on your purpose for reading. I usually try to read whole sentence of article, thus this advice changed my viewpoint.

Japanese language background tutors.

- I understand what one-to-one correspondence is.

Description of what went well or not so well

The data was classified into six themes, coded and instances of each code counted. The classifications emerging from these comments were: extremely positive comments, comments supporting the peer mentoring model of tutoring, comments regarding the tutor as a proofreader, editor or teacher rather than a peer mentor, affective factors influenced by the session, specific concerns regarding the session, and increased understanding of one's own weaknesses.

Comments supporting the peer mentoring model of tutoring were the most frequent type of comments. Such comments were made by 5% of tutees participating in sessions with English language background tutors and 5% of tutees participating in sessions with Japanese language background tutors. Examples of such comments follow:

English language background tutors.

- She did not just answer my questions. She gave me time to rethink my ideas and I could think by myself.

Japanese language background tutors.

- I like how we can discuss any topic that I want to know freely.
- Because the tutor always helps me to think about what I mean, I can think and understand the topic deeply.

Comments regarding the tutor as a proof-reader, editor or teacher rather than a peer mentor were the second most frequent type of comments. Such comments were made by 1% of tutees participating in sessions with English language background tutors and 4% of tutees participating in sessions with Japanese language background tutors. Examples of such comments follow:

English language background tutors.

- She explained what to consider while writing. Since it was so precise and easy to understand, her lecture seemed applicable to other essays in the future.
- She taught me how she edited my paper and why I need to revise my mistakes. I was surprized that she wrote down considerable amount of information on my hard copy and I was embarrassed that I did not prepare so much for her.

Japanese language background tutors.

- His lecture suited my needs and I could understand the whole contents of the target chapter.
- This tutor's way of teaching always makes me understand the exercises for this subject on my own, which is very motivating. He goes straight to the point that I do not understand and the speed is perfect for a one hour session. We cover a lot.

The influence of sessions on affective factors were the next most frequent type of comments. Such comments were made by 1% of tutees participating in sessions with English language background tutors and 3% of tutees participating in sessions with Japanese language background tutors. Examples of such comments follow:

English language background tutors.

- You explained really in detail about trigonometric functions. I am feeling a little more confident for tomorrow's class.

- When I read the feedback from my instructor, I completely lost my confidence, but after this session, I recovered it and modified my essay. I could ask not only spelling or grammatical accuracy, but also the problem from a native speaker's perspective.

Japanese language background tutors.

- I feel I am gradually gaining confidence in myself.
- This tutor has made me understand the concepts for this class in a simple and logical manner where I feel confident in approaching exercises in this topic without feeling like I don't understand at all.

Concerns regarding sessions were the next most frequent type of comments. Such comments were made by 3% of tutees participating in sessions with English language background tutors and <1% of tutees participating in sessions with Japanese language background tutors. Examples of such comments follow:

English language background tutors.

- I am not good at speaking English and sometimes I stopped my speaking during the session, but my tutor heard what I tried to say. The atmosphere was very comfortable.
- I talked more and she said less. I wanted her to be more active to give me tips for my essay, but by talking I think I got many information that can help my essay to improve, so I really appreciate it.
- I could understand about today's section, but study in English is super hard for me. Unfortunately, I'm not good at English so…
- I could learn new things from the tutor but sometimes I could not understand the tutor's points.

Japanese language background tutors.

- Just solving TOEFL problems is not a session, I can do that in my room. I want to focus more on why my answer is correct or not.

Extremely positive comments were the next most frequent type of comments. Such comments were not made by any tutees participating in sessions with English language background tutors, but they were made by 1% of tutees participating in sessions with Japanese language background tutors. Examples of such comments follow:

Japanese language background tutors.

- I could feel that she really likes mathematics, and she really understands the principles and important key points of mathematics so well.
- Everything was good!

The least frequent category of comments were comments relating to understanding one's weaknesses. Such comments were not made by any tutees participating in sessions with Japanese language background tutors, but they were made by 1% of tutees participating in sessions with English language background tutors. These three comments follow:

English language background tutors.

- I could understand the weaknesses of my paragraphs very clearly.
- I realized that I have a tendency to repeat the same thing in a different sentence so from now on I will not make the same mistake.
- I realized that I'm not good at grammar and I need to learn more grammar.

Discussion

Centre usage

The usage results seem to demonstrate that if student support services are offered in the context of an ETP in Japan, there is the potential for them to be well utilised by students over the long term. The finding that one in five students at the university who were not employed as tutors in the centre was a user of the support services on offer is promising for other universities, where the overall student population may be much larger, as it indicates that the establishment of support services is likely to be worth the substantial effort involved.

There are a large number of limitations with this research, which must be taken into account when considering the findings of the study. First and foremost, the study focussed on one academic support centre at a single, small university. The university curriculum is relatively challenging which may encourage higher usage rates (Bromley, Northway & Schonberg, 2013), since increasing academic achievement is a high priority for a large number of students within the context. At universities which are less academically challenging for students, usage rates may be lower.

All peer tutorial reservations are supposed to be made by tutees through the online tutorial reservation system. Attendance at sessions is also supposed to be recorded by the tutor for every tutorial session. In cases where the attendance field is left blank, the tutor is contacted by the centre co-ordinator and asked to record the attendance retrospectively. The usage data reported in this research assumes that all of these processes were followed without fail and that the sessions recorded on the online system are accurate. It is unlikely that additional sessions appear in the data which were not conducted. However, the opposite is quite likely; that some sessions were held which were not recorded correctly in the online system and therefore did not appear in the usage data reported here. Notwithstanding these limitations, conclusions can be drawn in terms of the extent to which there is potential for a peer support centre to be used in the context of an ETP in Japan.

The centre investigated in this chapter had been in operation for six years before the study was conducted. Other universities may be rightly concerned that if they establish a peer support service, it will be well used in the short term and then flounder once the novelty of the new offering has worn off. The usage rates shared in this study suggest that this is not the case. They suggest that even with little in the way of ongoing promotion of the service if the tutors are well trained and the quality of sessions is monitored, sustained demand is possible. Although clearly, the types of support for which there is demand will vary depending on the curriculum of the university.

Satisfaction and reported learning

The findings show that both tutors and tutees in the centre were satisfied with the experience and that tutees were more satisfied than tutors. This is also a promising result as the support services are offered for the benefit of tutees; it is the tutees' needs which are intended to be met through the tutorial sessions. On the other hand, tutors are employed to meet the needs of the tutees and are paid for their time and effort. Lansiquot and Rosalia (2015) have demonstrated that offering tutorial support enhances the academic achievement of tutors. This could be seen not as the primary aim of peer support services, but as a benevolent by-product and an advantage of peer support services over those offered by professional support staff. The high level of satisfaction in the sessions on the part of tutors revealed in this study could be seen in a similar light.

More careful consideration of the finding that tutees had significantly higher levels of satisfaction than tutors could offer several reasonable explanations. Firstly, one individual being willing to spend an hour of their time devoted to another individual and their problems is likely to be a relatively satisfactory experience for the receiver of support regardless of the giver's relative competence in all the many aspects of tutoring. Secondly, tutors have been trained for the position. They have a fairly detailed understanding of how the ideal peer support session should be offered through the training they have received. On the other hand, tutees sign up for sessions with no such understanding; they may have no understanding whatsoever of the nature of peer tutorial support or a limited understanding attained through previous sessions in the same centre. Therefore, tutees may be satisfied with the mere existence of such a support offering without considering too deeply the nature of such support, while tutors are likely to compare each session they offer to many aspects of the ideal peer support session that are discussed during the training they receive and may be aware of minor digressions from such training.

Perhaps the most illuminating result of this analysis was the analysis of the open-ended questions, the reports of tutors and tutees about the kinds of learning that they experienced during the tutorial sessions. Tutors gave a lot more specific reports of what they had learnt, whereas tutees often stated what they did during the session, or what aspects of the curriculum were covered without making specific reference to the learning they took away from the activity. This does not mean that tutors learnt more than tutees if anything the answers to the quantitative feedback questions suggest that tutees may have learnt more than tutors. What it does offer is greater insight into what the tutors perceive to have learnt than what the tutees do.

Although tutors are peers in one sense, peer tutors are usually more successful students than tutees, to begin with (often employed based on their academic record). As Harris (1992) stated, the training they receive to prepare for the position contributes to distancing them from their peers, giving them more of an educator role. The learning that has been found to occur during the peer tutorial sessions is likely to increase this distance with time spent in employment as they move further and further along the continuum from successful peer to educator while continuing to be called 'peer tutors'. Tutors' comments about their learning highlighted their movement along the continuum with a total of 1,023 examples of specific learning taking place during the 2,006 peer support sessions which would contribute to their increasing competence as peer tutors. This accumulated learning as they provide tutorial support during their employment could be considered to give them increasing insights into the process of education, thus strengthening their educator role and diminishing their role as peers.

Indeed, certain aspects of the peer tutoring position put peer tutors in a more privileged position to even classroom instructors. For example, tutees often share detailed accounts of what their classes (and instructors) are like and share the idiosyncrasies of their instructors' feedback and assessment practices. Peer tutors gain insight into what happens in each instructor's classes and can thus gain an overview of the range of different teaching styles and approaches that are in use across the university. This kind of insight is not readily available to most instructors. Teaching has been described as "the egg carton profession" (Lortie, 1975, p. 223) because each instructor works in their own classroom, quite isolated from other instructors and with little insight into what goes on in other instructors' classrooms.

Another kind of learning achieved frequently by tutors during their peer support sessions was increased learning about the subject in focus. The preparation for teaching/tutoring a peer is particularly effective for increasing the tutor's own understanding of the subject matter (Astin, 1993; Pascarella & Terenzini, 2005; Topping, 1996). In addition, in a peer mentoring model of tutoring, which is very tutee-centred and relies on active listening as the predominant tutoring activity, tutors may increase their understanding of a subject by hearing and being required to respond to a wide range of questions about each area of the subject in focus. As different learners think and approach problems differently, tutors are almost required to think about the subject and approach problems within the subject from a wide range of perspectives. In addition, the peer mentoring model will inevitably result in tutors being asked some questions that they cannot answer. Both approaches to answering such questions (demonstrating to the tutee a method of finding answers to such questions, or asking the tutee to find out the answer to their question and report back to the tutor in the subsequent session) will necessarily expand the tutor's knowledge of the subject in focus. As succinctly stated by Topping (1996, p. 324):

> Just preparing to be a peer tutor has been proposed to enhance cognitive processing in the tutor – by increasing attention to and motivation for the task, the necessitating of review of existing knowledge and skills. Consequently, existing knowledge is transformed by reorganization, involving new associations and a new integration. The act of tutoring itself involves further cognitive challenge, particularly with respect to simplification, clarification and exemplification.

There are limitations with this research, which must be taken into account when considering the findings of the study. The quantitative and qualitative data relating to the learning which took place during the peer support sessions were self-report data. Feedback was given confidentially at the end of each tutorial session, with both the tutor and tutee completing online questionnaires at the same time, in two separate rooms. The tutors and tutees were aware that the other party involved in the session would not read the responses. Nevertheless, tutees may have had a tendency to be overly complimentary about the tutor for fear of the tutor, their peer, being negatively evaluated by the centre management.

The most illuminating results of this analysis were the reports of specific learning which took place during sessions on the part of both tutors and tutees. When the decision was made to ask tutors and tutees to report what they learnt during their sessions, it was not anticipated that such a wide range of different dimensions of learning would be reported. The learning on the part of the tutees demonstrates that an academic support centre such as the one investigated here is beneficial for helping tutees to fill gaps in their knowledge, to review aspects of courses that they find challenging or difficult to understand, to gain additional practice in the kinds of activities that are required of them during homework assignments and tests and, perhaps most importantly, to receive confirmation that they are on the right track with their academic work. The learning on the part of tutors was especially broad, encompassing ever-increasing competence in tutoring skills, understanding of different learners, learning styles, strategies and study methods, and understanding of the curriculum at the university, especially with respect to the subject areas in which they were already successful. Disregarding the relative affordability of peer tutorial support over that which is offered by professional support staff, the extent to which mutual academic development appears to be possible for both tutors and tutees during a large majority of sessions suggests that establishing such a centre is well worth the time, effort and frustrations involved in the process.

Linguistic background of tutors

The first clear outcome of this comparison is that there is not a substantial difference between tutee satisfaction with tutors who have a Japanese language background versus those who have an English language background. No statistically significant difference was found between three out of four quantitative questions, and many of the comments provided by tutees who were supported by tutors with a Japanese language background were similar to those provided by tutees who have an English language background. In fact, the results of the first qualitative question, in which the tutees described what they had learnt during the session, were remarkably similar.

However, tutees do seem to be slightly more satisfied with the one-to-one tutorial sessions when those sessions are conducted by tutors with a Japanese language background. This is demonstrated by the statistically significant difference between the tutees overall satisfaction with the sessions based on language background, and different feelings that tutees reported in the qualitative data related to what went well or not so well in the session may help to explain that higher satisfaction.

The most frequent type of comments was those regarding the peer tutor, not as a peer, but in the role of an expert. Intuition might encourage us to think of Japanese language background tutors as closer to true peers and native English speakers as more distant language experts. However, contrary to this intuition, tutees more often referred to tutors with Japanese language background as experts. The language used in the comments; such as the word "lecture" and different forms of the word "teach", may express not a distant relationship like that between a teacher and student, but rather admiration and respect on the part of the tutee. This seems to illustrate the potential of educators with the same language background as students to strongly influence those students (Murphey, 1998).

Tutees who had sessions with Japanese language background tutors offered significantly more comments relating to increased confidence as those who had sessions with English language background students. This may relate to the effect of Near Peer Role Models (Murphey, 1998) on tutees' motivation. On the contrary, tutees who had sessions with English language background tutors were more likely to mention increased understanding of their own weaknesses. Although greater understanding of one's weaknesses can be the first stage in the process of developing learner autonomy (Reinders, 2010), there were no related comments from either group of tutees regarding increased understanding of their strengths, which could be equally useful in the process of becoming more autonomous. Moreover, the increased understanding of one's weaknesses, especially when expressed in isolation from an increased understanding of one's strengths, may have a detrimental effect on a learner's confidence.

The concerns expressed by tutees seemed to vary based on the language background of the tutor. Tutees who had Japanese language background tutors were significantly less likely to express concerns and when they did, the concerns focussed on practices during sessions that they found unproductive. On the other hand, tutees who had sessions with English language background tutors were ten times as likely to express concerns and their concerns were noticeably different in nature, predominantly expressing difficulties in communicating with the tutor due to different language backgrounds. This is similar to the finding of Park and Shin (2010) that having a shared dominant language can be a beneficial resource in the process of the tutee's learning.

Finally, extremely positive comments were only expressed by tutees who had had sessions with Japanese language background tutors. This would seem to indicate that those sessions were more likely to leave tutees feeling extremely satisfied with the support offered. Indeed, these students may have come away from their sessions feeling inspired (Murphey, 1998) by discussing academic topics with Near Peer Role Models who are academically successful.

In a previous study, Ruegg (2015) found that teacher feedback pushed students outside of their comfort zone, to increase their language output, whereas peer feedback pushed students to improve their language output, yet stayed within their comfort zone, resulting in fewer revision attempts but a higher level of success from each attempt. The qualitative analysis results in this chapter appear to be similar, albeit with English language background peer tutors taking the teacher role and Japanese language background peer tutors taking the peer role. It seems that the Japanese language background tutors more often leave their tutees feeling confident and motivated, while the English language background tutors more often push their tutees, to feel difficulty in their attempts to communicate, to understand their own weaknesses but ultimately to make clear areas for further improvement. It is unclear which approach to tutoring is likely to be more effective pedagogically. Which approach has a stronger effect may depend on each tutee's personality.

There are limitations with this analysis which affect the extent to which strong conclusions can be drawn and the generalisability of the findings. Firstly, although all tutees answered the quantitative feedback questions, not all tutees wrote qualitative comments. Therefore, the qualitative analysis necessarily only describes the feelings of those who chose to write comments. Furthermore, some comments were not terribly useful to include in such an analysis and were therefore excluded from the analysis resulting in a partial representation of tutee's views. For example, in response to the qualitative part of question two (describing what they learnt), one student wrote "Chapter 2". Although the session may have been pedagogically valuable for that tutee, there was simply not enough information to understand the kind of learning taking place. Furthermore, the data analysed in this chapter was from a single educational institution. Each institution has a certain institutional culture, thus the results may not be duplicated in a different institution. Nevertheless, there are some conclusions that can be drawn from these results, which may be useful for other institutions to consider in offering support outside of the classroom to students in EMI programmes in Japan and beyond.

One suggestion for further research in the area would be to conduct a similar study with deeper qualitative data, in the form of individual interviews with tutees, to gain a deeper understanding of their experiences during sessions and perceptions of different tutors. Another suggestion, which could be conducted in a large centre, or one that has a less linguistically mixed population than the centre under discussion here, would be to compare the satisfaction of tutees from different language proficiency levels with tutorials conducted by English language background tutors, as it would seem likely that the tutees who experienced difficulties in communicating with the English language background tutors had lower proficiency levels than those who did not. Determining the proficiency level at which the language background of the tutor ceases to be a problem would be a valuable contribution to the field.

There is no evidence in the results presented here to support the idea that native English speakers are more appropriate than Japanese students as tutors in the Japanese EMI context. If anything, the evidence suggests that as Near Peer Role Models, students with a traditional Japanese background may be more effective in offering support to fellow Japanese learners. However, in this regard, the results are mixed, with what appear to be more similarities than differences between the sessions offered by the two groups of tutors. Thus, as suggested by Park and Shin (2010, p. 114), "it seems worthwhile to maintain a balance of NESTs and NNESTs". One aspect of the results that does seem clear is that native English speaking tutors will not satisfy the needs of all tutees. Thus, employing tutors from a range of different language and educational backgrounds in support centres may increase the range of students who feel comfortable using support services in addition to making it easier to find students to employ in peer support roles in such centres.

References

Arum, R. & Roksa, J. (2011). *Academically adrift: Limited learning on college campuses.* University of Chicago Press.

Astin, A. (1993). *What matters in college: Four critical years revisited.* Jossey-Bass.

Banjong, D. (2015). International students' enhanced academic performance: Effects of campus resources. *Journal of International Students, 5*(1), 132–142.

Bradford, A. (2013). English-medium degree programs in Japanese universities: Learning from the European experience. *Asian Education and Development Studies, 2*(3), 225–240.

Bromley, P., Northway, K., & Schonberg, E. (2013). How important is the local really? A cross-institutional quantitative assessment of frequently asked questions in writing center exit surveys. *The Writing Center Journal, 33*(1), 13–37.

Bromley, P., Northway, K., & Schonberg, E. (2018). L2 student satisfaction in the writing center: A cross-institutional study of L1 and L2 students. *Praxis: A Writing Center Journal, 16*(1), 20–31.

Carino, P. (1995). Early writing centers: Toward a history. *The Writing Center Journal, 15*(2), 103–115.

Carson, J. G. & Nelson, G. L. (1994). Writing groups: Cross-cultural issues. *Journal of second language writing, 3*(1), 17–30.

Gofine, M. (2012). How are we doing? A review of assessments within writing centers. *The Writing Center Journal, 32*(1), 39–49.

Harris, M. (1992). Collaboration is not collaboration is not collaboration: Writing center tutorials vs. peer-response groups. *College Composition and Communication 43*(3), 369–383.

Holliday, A. (2006). Native-speakerism. *ELT Journal, 60*(4), 385–387.

Ishikura, Y. (2015). Realizing internationalization at home through English-medium courses at a Japanese university: Strategies to maximize student learning. *Higher Learning Research Communications, 5*(1), 11–28.

Kalikoff, B. (2001). From coercion to collaboration: A mosaic approach to writing center assessment. *Writing Lab Newsletter, 26*(1), 5–7.

Kelo, M. (2006). Support for international students in higher education: Practice and principles. *ACA papers on international cooperation in education*. Lemmens.

Kelo, M. & Rogers, T. (with Rumbley, L.) (2010). International student support in European Higher Education: Needs, solutions and challenges. *ACA papers on international cooperation in education*. Lemmens.

Kuh, G., Kinzie, J., Schuh, J., Whitt, E., et al. (2010). *Student success in college: Creating conditions that matter*. Jossey Bass.

Lansiquot, R. & Rosalia, C. (2015). Online peer review: Encouraging student response and development. *Journal of Interactive Learning Research, 26*(1), 105–123.

Lasagabaster, D. & Sierra, J. (2002). University students' perceptions of native and non-native speaker teachers of English. *Language Awareness, 11*(2), 132–141.

Leask, B. (2009). Using formal and informal curricula to improve interactions between home and international students. *Journal of Studies in International Education, 13*(2), 205–221.

LeClare, E. & Franz, T. (2013). Writing centers: Who are they for? What are they for? *SiSAL Journal, 4*(1), 5–16.

Lee, R. (1988). Assessing retention program holding power effectiveness across smaller community colleges. *Journal of College Student Development, 29*(3), 255–262.

Lortie, D. (1975). *Schoolteacher: A sociological study*. University of Chicago Press.

Macauley, W. (2012). Getting from values to assessable outcomes. In E. Schendel & W. Macauley (Eds.). *Building writing center assessments that matter* (pp. 25–56). Utah State University Press.

McKinley, J. (2010). English language writing centres in Japanese universities: What do students really need? *Studies in Self-Access Learning Journal, 1*(1), 17–31.

McKinley, J. (2011). Group workshops: Saving our writing centre in Japan. *Studies in Self-Access Learning Journal, 2*(4), 292–303.

Moust, J. & Schmidt, H. (1994a). Facilitating small-group learning: A comparison of student and staff tutors' behaviour. *Instructional Science, 22,* 287–301.

Moust, J. & Schmidt, H. (1994b). Effects of staff and student tutors on student achievement. *Higher Education, 28,* 471–482.

Murphey, T. (1998). Motivating with near peer role models. *On JALT97: Trends & Transitions,* 201–205.

North, S. (1984). The idea of a writing center. *College English, 46*(5), 433–446.

Okuda, T. (2019). Student perceptions of non-native English speaking tutors at a writing center in Japan. *Journal of Second Language Writing, 44,* 13–22.

Oley, N. (1992). Extra credit and peer tutoring: Impact on the quality of writing in introductory psychology in an OA college. *Teaching of Psychology, 19*(2), 78–81.

Park, S. & Shin, S. (2010). "She immediately understood what I was trying to say": Student perceptions of NNESTs as writing tutor pedagogy. *WATESOL NNEST Caucus Annual Review, 1,* 100–118.

Pascarella, E. & Terenzini, P. (2005). *How college affects students: A third decade of research.* Jossey-Bass.

Reinders, H. (2010). Towards a classroom pedagogy for learner autonomy: A framework of independent language learning skills. *Australian Journal of Teacher Education, 35*(5), 40–55.

Ruegg, R. (2015). Differences in the uptake of peer and teacher feedback on writing. *RELC Journal, 46*(2), 131–145.

Salem, L. (2016). Decisions… decisions: Who chooses to use the writing center? *The Writing Center Journal, 35*(2), 147–171.

Schendel, E. & Macauley, W. J. (2012). *Building writing center assessments that matter.* University Press of Colorado.

Thompson, G. (2014). Moving online: Changing the focus of a writing centre. *Studies in Self-Access Learning Journal, 5*(2), 127–142.

Thompson, I. (2006). Writing center assessment: Why and a little how. *The Writing Center Journal, 26*(1), 33–61.

Topping, K. (1996). The effectiveness of peer tutoring in further and higher education: A typology and review of the literature. *Higher Education, 32,* 321–345.

Trimbur, J. (1987). Peer tutoring: A contradiction in terms. *The Writing Center Journal 7*(2), 21–28.

Wilkinshaw, I. & Duong, O. T. H. (2012). Native- and non-native speaking English teachers in Vietnam: Weighing the benefits. *TESL-EJ The electronic journal of English as a Second Language, 16*(3), 1–17.

Williams, J. & Takaku, S. (2011). Help-seeking, self-efficacy, and writing performance among college students. *Journal of Writing Research, 3(1),* 1–18.

Zhao, Y. (2017). Student interactions with a native-speaker tutor and a non-native speaker tutor at an American university. *The Writing Center Journal, 36*(1), 57–87.

4 Guidelines for supporting EMI students outside of the classroom

Getting started

Determining the need for support

In order to determine the support needs in an educational institution, different kinds of information need to be collected and considered.

1. Collect information about the difficulties students face in the current curriculum. This information can be collected from students or instructors, but it will ideally be collected from both students and instructors.
   - Information can be collected from students through the use of questionnaires or interviews. One possibility is to target students who are struggling to collect this information, although there are strong arguments for trying to collect it from a cross-section of students with different levels of academic success.
   - Information can also be collected from instructors through the use of questionnaires and interviews. One possibility is to target instructors in courses with which students struggle more (which have lower grades). However, all instructors are likely to provide useful information about the difficulties faced by students in their courses.

   The difficulties that students may have with the curriculum should be considered as broadly as possible. All aspects of the curriculum should be asked about, including preparation for classes (reading), classroom interaction (both listening and speaking), course assignments (writing, presentations and tests) and any other skills that may be relevant, such as searching for materials on the internet or at the library, notetaking, referencing.

2. Find out ways in which real/perceived student weaknesses have limited the current curriculum. Instructors may have some ideal activities that they would like to include in their courses but do not because they do not feel the students would be able to complete them successfully. In addition, there may be activities that an instructor previously included in their course, but removed because they caused difficulty for students. Collecting information about these kinds of limitations are useful to inform support offerings that may be beneficial. If students can be supported to succeed in activities that they are not currently asked to complete because of real/perceived weaknesses, then the support can fill the role of scaffolding students to reach a higher potential.
3. Although it is unlikely, it is possible that students do not face any difficulties in the current curriculum and that instructors do not feel any limitations due to student weaknesses. In this case, instructors could be asked to consider a blue-skies activity in which they think of possible activities that would be useful in further extending students' competence in their subject area. Asking questions in this way may empower teachers to think outside the box when designing assignments.

Deciding the format of support

There is a range of different formats in which support can be offered. In order to decide which method/s is/are the most appropriate in a given context, I would recommend making an educated guess about which formats to adopt and starting with a small selection of different formats. Through time, formats can be stopped or changed and new formats can be offered in order to fill support needs. In particular, as instructors in particular subjects come and go from an institution, format changes are likely to be called for. The kinds of formats one may choose include:

1. Providing support within a course. This may involve support staff taking over some of the teaching time (as little as one lesson and as much as once per week) to visit the classroom and offer skills support. Alternatively, whole-class sessions could be organised in addition to the regular teaching time. If they are offered in addition, the course instructor will need to determine whether the sessions should be mandatory or optional.

    Such sessions should be focussed on particular academic skills required for the course, while the instructor teaches content. This distinction between academic skills and content is useful to avoid overlap between what is taught by the course instructor and the support staff while increasing the extent to which course instruction and support can complement each other. Such sessions could focus on:

- General skills required for the course,
- Specific skills required for a particular assignment/s,
- Study sessions in preparation for a test or examination.

Providing support within a course requires communication with the course instructor, to determine the support needs in the class and the timing and content of such support offerings. In the case that classroom instructors are not positive about the benefits of such support offerings, they are unlikely to be successful. Thus, it is recommended that courses be chosen carefully when considering embedding support within a course in this way.

Offering a one-off academic skills session related to a particular course can also be a useful method of introducing students to other formats of support offered outside of the classroom. Therefore, even if there is not much time for such sessions, a single session in a course can prove particularly beneficial if other formats of support are also on offer.

2. General skills workshops in a group format. Such workshops may be best to organise in the evenings or weekends and can run from one hour up to four hours. Students should be asked to sign up in advance for such workshops. This enables them to be cancelled if there is not enough interest and helps with the determination of the number of support staff required to run the workshop. In my experience, such sessions can be successful with as few as four students and one support staff member as well as with as many as 30 students and five support staff members. The following are examples of the kinds of skills on which workshops may focus:

- Time management skills
- Reading strategies
- Presentation skills
- Note-taking skills
- Standardised language test skills for TOEFL ITP, TOEFL iBT, IELTS, Cambridge or TOEIC (workshops may be offered for one particular section of a test, or for the test as a whole, specific workshops for the writing and speaking sections of tests may be especially useful.)

- Library research
- Writing strategies
- Paragraph writing
- Essay writing
- Research paper writing
- Timed writing

3. One-to-one tutorial support. This is usually the most popular format for support and the format for which there is most demand. However, this may vary depending on the context. This is the format which is the focus of chapter three of this book.
4. Drop-in desk. A drop-in desk (sometimes referred to as a help desk or a support desk) is a fixed location at which a support staff member is stationed, available to answer questions about homework or study skills.

The extent to which drop-in desks are used seems to vary drastically at different times of the semester. Thus, it may be useful to consider opening a drop-in desk at certain times of the semester rather than all year round. Especially at the end of the semester when students are preparing for tests and exams, there is likely to be high demand for support on a drop-in basis.

A single drop-in desk can be offered which is intended to provide support for all subjects and skills. However, finding appropriate staff for such a desk may be difficult. Other alternatives include providing support for different subjects on different days, or at different times of the day. It may also be found that there is support for a drop-in desk for some particular subjects. If this is the case, a drop-in desk for a specific subject may be offered. In particular, I have found that drop-in desks are useful for mathematics support as students often have quick questions with which they need help. On the other hand, with writing support, students often need more detailed guidance and a one-to-one tutorial session may be more appropriate.

Finding a venue

Finding a home for support services is another consideration once a need has been established. A drop-in desk is the easiest format of support space-wise, as very little space is required. A drop-in desk could be located in a lobby or even in a corridor. Other formats of support pose greater challenges, requiring more space. If you take the time to look back at the history of academic support centres, you will find that they often started out making do with a very small space. Once a service can demonstrate that there is a demand for the support they offer, this can be used to negotiate more space. In an ideal world, a comfortable space will be able to be found to start a support offering. It is much more likely that a small and uncomfortable space will be the starting point and that a centre will slowly grow, proving its worth and eventually securing a comfortable space. Fortunately, only enough space for a desk is really necessary to start a support service. Space may be found in the following places:

- In the library (if the library does not allow talking, a closed room within the library will be required)
- In a self-access centre
- In a classroom
- In an office.

Deciding details of support

The main details that need to be decided are the timing and duration and who will offer the support.

1. The timing and duration of support will depend partly on where the support is located. If the support is located in a place already frequented by students, such as in the library, a self-access centre or in a lobby or corridor, I would suggest observing the venue over a period of time to find out the days and times at which the largest number of students can be found there. Times at which the location is the busiest, are likely to be the most successful times to offer support. However, if the venue is at the end of a corridor, in a place which students do not frequent, the best approach may be trial and error.If only one-to-one tutorial support is to be offered, then the timing does not need to be predetermined, only the duration. Support staff can inform the coordinator of all the days and times they are available to offer support and all these available times can be offered on a sign-up sheet or online booking system, for tutees to reserve. In this way, support can be offered at a time that suits both the tutor and the tutee and no-one needs to be in the location when there is no demand for support.
2. The duration of support offerings will depend to a large extent on the language proficiency level of the students in the context. Students at lower proficiency levels tend to complete a larger number of shorter tasks, thus requiring short and more frequent

sessions. For example, students who are studying a language at a lower proficiency level, rather than studying in the medium of a language, may write paragraphs rather than essays and practice speaking through short dialogues rather than long conversations. Such students may require sessions as short as ten minutes in duration and as long as 30 minutes. Once students reach a proficiency level at which they are capable of studying through the medium of English, they are likely to complete a smaller number of longer tasks, which may require longer support sessions. Such students are likely to require sessions ranging from around 45 minutes in duration to two hours. Students at higher levels, such as those studying in the fourth year and at postgraduate level, will complete tasks that are longer yet, such as theses and full-length presentations. These students will require longer sessions and possibly require multiple sessions for a single task. These students are likely to require sessions at least one hour in length.

3. Another detail that needs to be decided is who will offer the support. Four main types of support staff should be considered.

- Professional support staff. Professional support staff are the best option if it is important that support staff be available at all times. Because professional support staff are paid well for this position, they can be expected to be available. On the other hand, the biggest disadvantage of professional support staff is the cost. If plenty of funding is available and the funding available can increase through time as the need for support grows, then this option should be seriously considered. However, funding may make this option impossible.
- Academic staff who teach in the institution. If academic staff are also employed as support staff, the ideal arrangement is that a fixed number of hours in the support centre each week can replace one course. For example, in lieu of a course which has 3 contact hours per week, an academic staff member could be asked to spend a fixed number of hours per week in the support centre (probably somewhere in the range of six to nine hours). Such an arrangement demonstrates the importance of this task to the instructors involved and balances the workload between those who offer support and those who do not.

  Even if there is insufficient support from the institution's management to offer such an arrangement, academic staff may still be a viable option for support offerings. There are many examples of support services being started through the dedication of a small number of instructors who are willing to volunteer their free time to support students outside of their own classes. Even as few as two instructors who are willing to do this may be enough to get a support service started, in institutions at which instructors are required to have office hours, a larger number of instructors may volunteer to conduct their office hours in a specific location and allow students from other classes to visit them as well as their own students.

- Graduate students who are studying at the institution. Graduate students could be employed as support staff and paid for the position if some funding is available for such a service, but not enough funding to cover the high cost of professional support staff.

  If funding is not available, another option for employing graduate students is an arrangement by which they receive course credit in return for offering a fixed amount of academic support to other students. This could be considered as a course, in which students receive training at the beginning of the semester and then offer support for a fixed number of hours over the remainder of the semester in order to pass the course and receive credit. They could also be asked to write a final reflection or report on their experiences of offering academic support and this could constitute a final graded assignment.

  Another option for employing graduate students when neither funding nor credit is available is for students to offer academic support on a voluntary basis. I would suggest that if students are volunteering their time, they should be rewarded with a certificate in appreciation of their work. This provides evidence of their service to the institution, which can be included in their resumes to help with job hunting.

- Undergraduate students who are studying in the institution. The three main options available for employing undergraduate students as peer tutors are the same as the options for graduate students: they can be employed and paid for the work, can be offered course credit for the work, or they can work on a voluntary basis and receive recognition of the work. In the case of peer tutors who are themselves, undergraduate students, the hourly rate of pay can be less than that paid to a graduate student. Therefore, undergraduate students are the most cost-effective of the paid alternatives. It may also be easier to negotiate a credit-bearing academic support course for undergraduate students as the curriculum tends to be more flexible than that of graduate students. Moreover, since the job hunting process is more difficult for those with undergraduate degrees than for those with postgraduate degrees, a certificate of service may be more coveted by undergraduate students than by their postgraduate counterparts. If funding is not available and it is difficult to recruit volunteers, it may be useful to consider approaching students in a teacher licensing, teacher education, or other education-related programme, as students in such programmes are more likely to value the work experience offered by a voluntary academic support role.

Creation of support policies

Support service policies can and should be changed over time to ensure that they are fit for purpose. However, it is important to create an initial set of policies before a support service is offered, to ensure that there is some clarity about what kind of support the centre is to offer and how it is to offer it. There are three main types of policies that need to be considered:

1. Policies to prevent plagiarism. One of the greatest risks involved in offering support outside of the classroom is the possibility of plagiarism. That is, the support staff provides too much support to students, to a point where the work could no longer be said to be the student's work. No support staff member intends to do this, but a desire to be helpful can result in unintentional plagiarism. There is a range of different policies that can help to prevent plagiarism in support service contexts, such as:

    • Always maintaining a focus on the development of the student receiving support rather than the piece of work under discussion. The intention should be to focus primarily on the student's learning and the piece of work under discussion should be seen as a vehicle through which such learning can occur. Another way of seeing this is that attention should be focussed on the processes used by the student in creating the final product, rather than on the final product they come up with.
    • Support staff could be forbidden from picking up a pen/pencil during support sessions. This is a commonly used policy in Writing Centers to prevent tutors from unintentionally writing

their own words on the student's work. This policy alone is not likely to be completely effective. Dictating information for students to write should also be discouraged. If support is offered online, the equivalent policy would be that explanations can be typed, rather than the answer and support staff should ensure that an answer (or a correct version) is never provided in what they type. In the example of writing, rather than correcting a student's writing, the tutor would be asked to locate problems and provide comments in the margins which explain why they are problematic, rather than providing a revised version.
- Wherever possible, offering two alternative options to address a problem in a student's work. This policy can be difficult in support for subjects such as mathematics where there is usually only one way to arrive at the answer but is particularly useful for language-related support where there are invariably more than one grammatical structures, more than one word and more than one way of organising an essay or a presentation that would be effective.

2. Policies to ensure that support services are conducted in an ethical way. There is a wide range of possible ethical policies, such as:
   - Support staff always provide support services only in the support centre and during the centre's operating hours.
   - Support staff not providing support to anyone with whom they are in a relationship.
   - Students having the right to request a different support staff member at any time.
   - Complete confidentiality for students in terms of what is discussed during support sessions.

3. Language policies. Suitable language policies are not so clear cut, rather what is suitable will depend to a great extent on the context and in particular the language policies of the institution and the institutional culture surrounding language use. Although it may seem counterintuitive, my experience is that institutional policies and especially institutional culture are far more important in deciding appropriate language policies than the language proficiency levels of students in the institution. Policies that align with institutional policy and especially institutional culture are significantly more likely to be followed. The main consideration when deciding language policies for a support service is to aim to make the service as student-centred as possible:

- To the extent possible, students who receive support should determine the language in which they should receive the support.
- Support staff should never feel that they are obliged to get a student to a point where they will pass their course. Rather, the goal should be to move students in the right direction towards eventual success. For a student who is unable to understand any of the course content due to insufficient language proficiency or large gaps in background knowledge, reaching a point where they understand just the key concepts of a course should be seen as a success, although this is unlikely to be enough progress for them to pass the course. Being student-centred should allow support staff to focus on the student's current capability and the next steps in their development.

Day to day operations

Recruiting student tutors

If postgraduate or undergraduate students are employed to offer support services, recruitment will need to occur more often as students may only be able to work in support positions for one to two years depending on their programme of study. In addition, a larger number will need to be employed, as they will be studying at the same time and therefore will not be able to work full-time in the centre. For these reasons, the employment of students means that recruitment of support staff becomes a part of the day to day operations of the centre. Processes for student recruitment are outlined below.

1. Appropriate selection criteria need to be decided upon, with which to communicate the kinds of students who are sought as well as to evaluate candidates once they apply. Criteria should focus on the following kinds of skills:
    - High motivation for the work
    - Strong interpersonal skills
    - An active and independent learner
    - Strong academic record (but not necessarily a top scholar)

2. An e-mail should be sent to all students in the relevant student population. (e.g. all undergraduate students, all postgraduate students, or all students). The e-mail should explain what the

position involves, the selection criteria, what application documents are required and a deadline for applications. The deadline for applications should be set early so that time remains for further recruitment activities if insufficient numbers of students apply. Application documents could include the following:

- An expression of interest (explaining their reasons for applying for the position)
- A cover letter (explaining why they think they would be a good candidate for the position)
- A resume (explaining previous work experience)
- The name and contact details of a referee who teaches within the institution (who can be contacted for further insight into the applicant's active and independent learning skills)
- Proof of English language proficiency
- A transcript of academic record (listing courses taken and grades)

3. If there are more than enough applicants to fill the required positions, priority may be given to the following types of applicants:

    - Those who can support a larger number of subject areas or skills
    - Those who will be able to work in the centre for longer once trained
    - Those who demonstrate high motivation

    This reduces the amount of effort required in the future to recruit and train more support staff due to need for support in different subjects, the student becoming unavailable because of job hunting or graduation or the student discontinuing the work once employed.

4. If there are not enough applicants to fill the required positions, the following further actions can be taken in efforts to recruit more applicants.

    - Visit relevant courses (such as teacher licensing courses, teacher education courses or other education-related courses) to answer questions students may have about the work and encourage students to apply.
    - E-mailing instructors to ask them to recommend students who they consider to be suitable candidates for the position. Be sure to outline the criteria for the position and stress that

academic excellence is not the primary consideration. For example, students who are active and collaborative in the classroom and who work well in groups may be better suited to support roles than those who are less active, less collaborative or find it difficult to get along with others despite receiving excellent grades. Such students can then be e-mailed directly, asking them whether they'd be interested in such a position.

Tutor training or orientation

If professional support staff or academic staff members are employed to provide support, then an orientation session will be required before they begin the work. On the other hand, if postgraduate or undergraduate students are employed, then a full training programme will be required. On orientation session may be as short as one hour and could be as long as four hours. In an orientation session, staff should be introduced to the purpose and philosophy of the centre, the processes and procedures for arranging and conducting sessions and the centre policies should be introduced and explained. Any kind of students who are employed as providers of support will require much more detailed preparation for the role. Such training will require at least four hours and as much as 15 hours – examples of the kinds of activities that can make up an academic support training programme follow.

1. Introduce tutors to the purpose and philosophy of the centre.
2. Discussion of the role of a peer tutor. Including both what the role entails and the limits of the role. For example, tutors are not psychologists and should not attempt to help students with psychological problems. However, they should be made aware of the services available on campus so that they can refer students to another service to get the help they need.
3. Understanding different kinds of learners. Peer tutors should realise what kind of learner they are and become aware of a wide range of different kinds of learners. They should also become aware of different conceptions of education that students from different cultural and socioeconomic backgrounds might have. Scenarios can be discussed involving different kinds of learners and the approaches to learning a particular subject that might be appropriate for those learners. Tutors should reach an

understanding that what works for them as a learner might not work for others and the need to be open-minded when dealing with others.
4. If peer tutors will be offering one-to-one tutorial sessions, they should be introduced to the tutoring cycle (MacDonald, 2000) and should practice different stages of the cycle in role plays.
5. Students should learn about and practice using active listening skills, including nonverbal and minimal encouragers. It may also be useful to discuss eye contact as this is something that students may have difficulty balancing. A useful activity is to have students practice active listening skills in groups of three. One student talks about something important to them, another student actively listens and a third student observees the communication and records what they see. At the end of a specified period of time (perhaps around five minutes), the talker and listener discuss how the communication went for each of them and the observer reports anything they noticed about the listener's active listening skills.
6. Discussion of Tutor Talking Time (TTT) (MacDonald, 2000): Why tutors should talk as little as possible during academic support sessions and strategies for encouraging others to talk more. For example, the kinds of questions that can be asked to encourage students to reflect on their own learning rather than to depend on the tutor for explanations.
7. Processes and procedures for arranging and conducting sessions should be introduced and policies should be explained and discussed.

Once students have received introductory training in these kinds of topics, they should ideally observe at least one support session offered by another tutor. Following that they should ideally either have their first session observed by someone or record it for someone to watch. Either being observed or recorded is an important opportunity to receive feedback on their support. In the centre discussed in chapter three, tutors-in-training observed one session offered by a continuing tutor and then spent time discussing the session they had observed with the tutor before writing an observation report. Following that, they were observed by a continuing tutor as they conducted their first support session and spent time discussing their first session with that tutor before writing a reflection on their first session. The continuing tutor who observed their first session also wrote a report on how that first session went. The coordinator read the two observation reports and the reflection before the tutor-in-training had a final meeting with the coordinator to discuss their perspective on the two sessions (observed and conducted). The reports, the reflection and the discussion about the two sessions were the main mechanisms through which the coordinator determined whether the tutor-in-training was ready to be employed in a support role.

In addition to the above training, tutors-in-training might be encouraged to read some of the sources of information listed in the bibliography. Using chapters from books such as these, and/or other materials, tutor training can be expanded into a semester-long credit-bearing course.

Promotion

Support services will need to be promoted regularly in order to ensure that awareness of the support offerings is maintained. Ideally, support services will be promoted to both staff and students. Although students are the users of support services, staff are useful in mentioning appropriate support services to specific students at appropriate points in time. There are three main methods of promoting support services to staff and students:

1. Sending an e-mail to staff and students. An e-mail can be sent to all staff at the beginning of each semester, encouraging them to encourage specific students to make use of support services. Although this may not be an effective promotion technique in a large institution, as staff are likely to receive large numbers of e-mails. An e-mail should be sent to all students at the beginning of each semester, informing them of the range of support services available in that semester and dates (if they are available).
2. Posters and screens. Posters and screen around campus can be used to promote support services. It may be especially useful to put them up near or inside the library.
3. Face-to-face promotion of support services is the most effective form of promotion. It may be especially effective if the providers of support themselves introduce the support offerings, rather than university administrative staff or the centre coordinator. I found it especially effective to visit the orientation for new first-year students each time it was offered as well as the orientation for incoming international students. In addition to that, specific courses with which support offerings may be helpful, such as those heavy in writing, can be visited by tutors towards the

beginning of each semester to quickly introduce the support services on offer. Especially in the case where students are employed to offer peer support, students meeting the peer supporters may increase the extent to which they find the support approachable.

Mentoring

Regardless of who is employed to offer support services, the support staff will require mentoring. However, in the case of postgraduate or undergraduate students being employed to provide support mentoring is especially important. Students may not have any previous experience working so closely with other people and are likely to face challenging situations that they are unsure how to deal with. It is important that they have someone they can turn to for advice as well as to talk through situations with after they have finished. The following are the kinds of mentoring that may be useful.

1. An open-door policy or office hours dedicated to supporting support staff.
2. Peer support groups organised and run by peers themselves. The groups can be set up at the beginning of the semester and a group organiser assigned. The purpose of the peer support groups should be explained to support staff for them to be successful. Groups may share issues that they have been having, share good ideas and strategies for effective support and such groups also provide an opportunity for them to ask each other questions about aspects of support offerings.
3. Periodically, other events should be held at which the whole support team can get together and build community. For example, there may be a social gathering at the end of each semester.

These kinds of mentoring and community building may be especially beneficial in cases where students are employed to provide peer support as they help to increase the desirability of the role and thereby increase the number of students who apply for positions.

Maintenance

There are maintenance activities that are also best considered on an ongoing basis. Activities to maintain support services include:

1. Reviewing and revising policies to be positioned at the balancing point between student wants and practices which are educationally effective. When there is a consideration of changing a policy, support staff can provide useful input into how the policy works for them and suggestions for improvement.
2. All formats of support should be monitored to determine changes to support offerings. For example, the timing and duration of support offerings may be reviewed. It is useful for support staff to always keep a record of usage rates of support services. If support services are well used on certain days but less used on other days, offerings could be tailored to better match student needs.
3. It is useful to have a kick-off meeting at the start of each semester for tutors who are continuing work in the centre. This meeting is a chance to communicate any changes to policies or centre procedures, as well as to set up peer support groups and assign leaders.

Enhancement

Review and evaluation

Based on usage data, it may be found that certain formats of support are unpopular and it may be prudent to discontinue certain offerings. However, before discontinuing support offerings review and evaluation should take place.

1. It is important to determine whether sufficient promotion has been conducted, as the reason for low usage rates may be that staff and students are not sufficiently aware of the offering rather than that there is no demand for the offering. This kind of feedback can be gathered through the use of simple questionnaires such as a poll on a social media site or the university website's student interface.
2. It is also possible that the format of support is demanded, but there may be problems with the way it is currently offered. In order to find out how effective the users of the support find the support to be, it may be beneficial to collect feedback from users. Such feedback could focus on whether they plan to use the offering again in the future, what they like about the offering and anything they feel should be changed. Such feedback could be printed on a piece of paper and handed to students as they leave the centre, provided at the door on a device or sent to student users via e-mail after their visit.

3. Collecting feedback from support staff who offer the service may also prove informative. Support staff may hear feedback directly from users while they are using the service that may be applied to improve the offering rather than discontinuing it.

Even for formats of support that are popular, collecting informal feedback may be effective to make improvements to support offerings. Feedback may be collected intermittently or systematically. Feedback such as that reported in chapter three may be useful to support increased or continued funding or space.

Additions

In addition to reviewing and evaluating the timing, duration, and format of services offered, additional aspects of support could be added to the existing support offerings. One way of receiving input on useful additions to the centre is to install a suggestions box in the centre in which support staff and users can make recommendations. The following additions are examples:

1. Purchasing reference books to keep in the centre. Such books can be referred to during support sessions but may also be used by students for self-study. Once a bookshelf is installed in the centre, support staff and students may make recommendations of books to purchase and add to the shelf.
2. A collection of information about a wide range of courses at the institution. Assignment description sheets and assessment rubrics or criteria may be especially useful to refer to during support sessions. They may be compiled in a folder or posted on the walls.

Professional development of tutors

Other additions can be made to centre offerings that would simultaneously supplement the support offerings as well as providing professional development opportunities for support staff. Support staff may be involved in creating feedback instruments used for review and evaluation of support offerings. Other additions that were made in the centre discussed in chapter three were:

1. Posters for promotion of support offerings were designed by peer tutors.
2. One peer tutor recorded and created a tutor training video that

demonstrated the tutoring cycle to be used in tutor training sessions.
3. A group of peer tutors created a set of self-study materials. The materials were kept on the desk in the centre and could be picked up by users of support services as well as non-users, thus increasing the study support available to both users and non-users of the centre as well as providing a professional development opportunity for peer tutors. The peer tutors decided which skills would be useful to cover in such materials and created a draft of each material which was reviewed by the centre coordination before being printed and shared in the centre. Topics covered included:

- Organisation in writing
- Proofreading and editing your writing
- In-text citations and referencing
- Strategies for timed writing tests
- Strategies for interview tests
- Strategies for reading tests

4. Peer tutors offered presentations about the support centre at local, national and international conferences.
5. Peer tutors wrote about the centre and published that writing. Students could write reflective essays, reports or research articles and they could be published on the institution's website, in a student journal and/or in national or international journals.

Bibliography

Fitzgerald, L. & Ianetta, M. (2016). *The oxford guide for writing tutors*. Oxford University Press.

Gillespie, P. & Lerner, N. (2008). *The Longman guide to peer tutoring*. Pearson Education.

Harris, M. (1995). Talking in the middle: Why writers need writing tutors. *College English*, 57(1), 27–42.

Lipsky, S.A. (2011). *A training guide for college tutors and peer educators*. Pearson Education.

Little, D. (1991). *Learner autonomy: Definitions, issues and problems*. Authentic Language Learning Resources Ltd.

Little, D. (1991). *Learner autonomy 2: Learner training for language learning*. Authentic Language Learning Resources Ltd.

MacDonald, R. B. (2000). *The master tutor: A guidebook for more effective tutoring*. Cambridge Stratford Ltd.

Murphy, C. & Sherwood, S. (2011). *The St. Martins sourcebook for writing tutors.* Bedford/St. Martins.

Newton, F. & Ender, S. (2010). *Students helping students: A guide for peer educators on college campuses.* Jossey Bass.

Ryan, L. & Zimmerelli, L. (2009). *Bedford guide for writing tutors.* Bedford/St. Martins.

Wood, D. & Wood, H. (1996). Vygotsky, tutoring and learning. *Oxford Review of Education, 22*(1), 5–16.

5 Conclusion: Supporting EMI students

The purpose of this book was to shed light on the important issue of supporting EMI students outside of the classroom. The questionnaire data reported in chapter two aimed to provide an overview of the kinds of support currently offered in universities with ETPs in Japan. Chapter three aimed to introduce one particular academic support centre for students in a full-degree EMI programme and consider the potential for such a centre to be used. The chapter added to this by considering whether such a centre is useful to students' learning. Finally, the chapter evaluated the relative effectiveness of tutorial sessions provided by peer tutors from traditional Japanese educational backgrounds compared to those with English as a first language. Chapter four is a collection of guidelines for setting up, maintaining and improving upon an academic support centre.

Several points from chapter two are worth discussing here. Firstly, according to the survey participants, there are no ETPs which consist solely of either Japanese domestic students or international students. Although the ratios of each vary greatly between institutions, ETPs in Japan are composed of a combination of both domestic and international students. Notably, 50% of the participants reported that 1–20% of students are Japanese domestic students, while the majority are international. The other 50% reported that 40–99% of students are Japanese domestic students, while there are also some international students present. This demonstrates that whatever support is offered needs to be appropriate to effectively support both domestic and international students.

In terms of the support offered, a notable trend was seen for older, more established EMI programmes to provide support at higher rates than newer programmes, especially those established in the last three years. The most frequent kind of support offered was writing skills support, while reading skills support was the least frequent. Moreover, all universities offering reading skills support were older, more established universities. The findings suggest that ETPs which have been established for longer have found support outside of the classroom to be necessary and have found reading skills support to be necessary and have thus added to their support offerings. This is helpful information for new programmes which may find it effective to ensure the availability of support outside of the classroom at the outset to avoid problems that a lack of support might create. Importantly, it may be useful to provide support for reading skills. Finally, there was a clear trend for support to be offered by university instructors, professional support staff and/or international students. On the other hand, few participants reported that Japanese students are employed as providers of support. Since research has found that providers of peer support learn as much as or more than, receivers of such support, it would seem that Japanese students are missing out on an opportunity for learning by not being considered for employment in peer support positions. In addition, tutees who participated in tutorial sessions with Japanese language background tutors were found to be significantly more satisfied with the sessions they participated in. Therefore, both potential tutors and tutees would appear to be disadvantaged by the lack of Japanese language background tutors.

The academic support centre usage data reported in chapter three demonstrated that it is possible to create a peer support centre that would be well utilised in the Japanese context, even with little in the way of marketing. Indeed, employing students to offer peer support rather than employing professional support staff or instructors in such roles may decrease the need for explicit marketing, as there is likely to be word-of-mouth marketing between tutors who work in the centre and other students who may subsequently use the centre. This may be an advantage of employing a larger number of students as peer tutors, although peer support will also increase the time required for recruiting, training and mentoring tutors.

In many contexts, L2 students have been found to have significantly higher uptake of support services than students whose L1 is the language of instruction. There is little research evidence available about the uptake of support services in EMI programmes, especially in the Japanese context. However, since in most EMI contexts the majority of students are non-native speakers of English, the overall usage rates would likely be higher in EMI contexts than in contexts where the local language is also the language of instruction. Indeed, one study that was conducted in an ETP in Japan by McKinley (2010) found usage rates that were higher than many other studies, which have usually been conducted in countries where the local language is also the medium of instruction. Although the evidence is limited, it suggests that there is the potential for high uptake of support services in EMI contexts. The usage found in the peer support centre discussed in chapter three supports this assumption, finding that over 2,000 tutorial sessions were carried out over an academic year with 156 tutees. Not only did one in five students use the centre during the year in question, but on average, the users participated in 13 tutorial sessions during the one-year period. These usage figures seem to show not only that a high number of students used the centre, but also that the students who did use the centre seem to have found it beneficial.

Chapter three corroborates the idea that the centre may bring benefits to users by reporting on user satisfaction rates. The satisfaction rates were very positive. However, students may have provided positive responses as a way of being polite. I believe that the average user returning to the centre 13 times over the year is a stronger indicator of user satisfaction than any numerical survey response can provide. It seems likely that if a student did not see benefit in a service after using it once or twice, they would not use their free time to continue signing up for and attending tutorial sessions.

Moreover, the qualitative survey results, describing what both tutors and tutees learnt during tutorial sessions, illustrate the benefits of participating in peer tutorial sessions more clearly. Tutors reported learning about their tutees, learning about the subject matter they were offering support for, learning about particular strategies or methods used by tutees and increased understanding of the curriculum of the university. The tutees reported learning about the subject matter in focus, learning strategies or study methods, learning specific language features, and increasing confidence in the subjects they were studying. This qualitative data shows both the breadth and depth of learning achieved by both tutors and tutees during peer tutorial sessions.

University teaching staff and professional support staff seem to be quite often engaged in this role in the Japanese context. There are certainly benefits to this, especially for institutions that have plenty of funding available. However, it is unquestionable that peer support services can be offered considerably more cheaply than professional support services, if not for free. While less funding is required, utilising students in the provision of support requires more time commitment from the head of the centre. Students need to be recruited, trained and mentored throughout their tenure. Moreover, students will not stay employed in the centre for as long as professional support staff would, so recruitment needs to occur more often. Furthermore, since most students are not available to work a large number of hours while studying full time, a larger number of students need to be recruited each time. Despite all the additional time required to operate a successful peer support centre, I believe that the double learning effect of tutors and tutees both learning from the peer tutorial sessions make it worthwhile, especially for institutions with a lack of funding for support services. It is also quite likely that the usage rates that can be achieved with peer support services are significantly higher as peers are likely to be seen as more approachable and less intimidating. In this way, peer support may increase the number of students learning from the support services in two ways: Not only tutees but also tutors appear to learn from the experience, and more tutees may visit the centre thus further increasing the number of students benefiting from the centre.

The final point addressed in chapter three was the issue of the linguistic background of peer tutors. The results of chapter two indicate that international students are employed to provide "peer" support services more than Japanese domestic students are in full degree EMI programmes in Japan. It would seem unfortunate that the benefits of being a tutor are not made available to Japanese students. In addition, the qualitative data discussed in chapter three suggest that not only the potential tutors but also tutees may be disadvantaged by this decision. Specifically, some tutees mentioned communication difficulties with native-English speaking tutors, which could lead to less effective sessions if serious and are likely to decrease students' confidence. Furthermore, students who participated in tutorial sessions with Japanese speaking tutors were more likely to end the sessions with increased feelings of confidence. Overall, there appear to be advantages to employing both Japanese students and international students in the provision of support services.

Implications

Providing support allows teachers to teach content that is more challenging. More challenging content, in turn, allows for greater learning to take place, more individual academic growth in each student through to graduation. If support is not offered, there are some options: individual support can be provided to students in teachers' offices outside of class time to allow all students to keep up, higher failure rates can be accepted in courses, or the curriculum can be simplified to ensure that it is achievable without support by all students. Literature on EMI in Japan would suggest that in many cases course content is kept simple to allow a wider range of students to succeed. I would suggest that being able to provide challenging content to students is important not only to increase the amount of learning that can be achieved but also to maintain students' motivation and passion for learning. A certain level of simplification of material to facilitate students' understanding is desirable, but if material is simplified too much, I believe the biggest risk is students becoming bored.

I would encourage any institution considering setting up an EMI programme, as well as any institution that already has an EMI programme to set up academic support services as early as possible, to provide the kinds of support that will enhance students success. Such support services should be responsive to the academic needs of students. One way of being responsive is to set up flexible support, to begin with, and then increase support in the areas where demand is found. Students could be asked about their difficulties in their course work and their needs for support. Similarly, teachers could be asked in what respects weaknesses in students' academic abilities cause difficulties in effective teaching of their courses. If an institution is serious about supporting students, they could even incorporate such questions into their course evaluation questionnaires, or conduct an additional questionnaire asking about students' support needs at the close of each semester.

EMI programmes in Japan are a unique educational context. It is important that support offerings are conceptualised and implemented in a way that is appropriate to this unique context. Literature on supporting students in Japan demonstrates that support offerings tend to follow one of two models. The first model reproduces support offerings that have successfully supported Japanese students' language skill development in the context of foreign language education. The second model reproduces support offerings that have successfully supported academic skills development in Anglophone contexts (invariably in North America, where such offerings have a longer history). Although aspects of both of these models are appropriate for the Japanese EMI context, neither of these models alone is sufficient to effectively support student success in this unique context.

Support offerings which have been successful in supporting Japanese students in foreign language skill development are different from the support required to successfully support students in EMI contexts in several ways. The most important difference is the significantly higher language proficiency level required to study in an EMI programme. Students in EMI programmes not only require a high English language proficiency level, but they also need a wider repertoire of skills and a higher level of fluency if they are to manage to successfully interact in

EMI classrooms, produce presentations and written assignments for EMI courses and keep up with the receptive language skills required to listen to and understand classes and to complete course readings. Another important difference between these contexts that has sometimes been overlooked is the requirement to develop, or further advance academic language skills as opposed to general language skills. Whereas general English language classes may include language used in casual, day-to-day contexts, academic English language classes focus on language skills necessary for academic contexts, such as understanding lectures and academic texts, formal presentation skills and writing formal academic essays. In addition to language skills, English for academic purposes programmes often aim to develop other skills such as critical thinking, logic and note-taking. The third major difference is the multicultural and multilingual make-up of the student body in EMI programmes. The results reported in chapter two demonstrate that all EMI programmes in Japan are made up of both international and domestic students to a greater or lesser extent. It could be expected that students who pay the same tuition fees should have the same kinds of services available to them. It would seem unethical to accept international students into a programme without providing academic support to them. Since such students may not be competent users of Japanese, this means that support needs to be available in English-medium. Moreover, this applies not only to international students, some Japanese domestic students may be returnees who have spent most or all of their lives overseas. Such students may also have insufficient Japanese language proficiency to function effectively in the academic context.

Support offerings which have been successful in supporting academic skills development in Anglophone contexts also have aspects which will be useful to apply in the Japanese EMI context, but applying them wholesale will not be sufficient in this unique context. Academic skills support services are usually designed specifically to address differences between secondary education and tertiary education in the geographical location where the support services are offered. In Anglophone contexts, this may involve changing from a more conversational and colloquial informal writing style to a more formal academic register. These services are also developed based on an assumption of oral fluency and lagging academic literacy skills. This is often the case for both English L1 students and English L2 students in Anglophone contexts. For example, L2 students in North America include a large number of refugee background students and generation 1.5 students, who are often fluent orally and aurally, whereas their English literacy skills have lagged behind. Specific practices which have come to be recognised as good practice in the context of writing centres, such as asking students to read their own writing aloud in order for them to catch problems, are likely to be less effective in the Japanese context because students are less likely to have oral fluency and lagging academic literacy skills. Rather, in the Japanese context, many students have highly developed academic literacy skills but less oral and aural fluency.

Since EMI programmes in Japan may include EAP preparation and/or sheltered instruction as well as content instruction in English-medium, a wider range of support offerings are likely to be required than in most other contexts. Through the conceptualisation, implementation and evolution of support services offered in EMI programmes in Japan, it is important for centre directors to pay careful attention to input from both students and teachers in order to be responsive to the particular needs of the wide range of students in the institution, and to changes in such needs throughout their academic journey.

Ongoing challenges

One of the main challenges facing EMI programmes in Japan is the availability of teaching staff who are experts in their subject area and are capable of teaching their subject area in the medium of English. Moreover, since these teachers need to teach their subject matter in English to a diverse group of students from different cultural, educational and language backgrounds, ideally they need not only expertise in their subject area and competence in the English language, but also a high level of intercultural communication skills to effectively reach those diverse students. The availability of professional support staff who can offer support for English-medium courses is also a challenge. For professional support staff too, a certain level of subject knowledge and a high level of English language proficiency are prerequisites and ideally, they too would have language education expertise or at least strong intercultural communication skills. One of the respondents to the questionnaire discussed in chapter two mentioned that "The university support staff in charge of international students do not speak English." Students who have been successful in taking EMI courses in the same programme have an appropriate level of subject knowledge and English language proficiency to support students who take those courses in the following semester or the following year. Thus, peer support would seem to be a good solution to this problem of finding suitable staff for support services.

Conclusion: Supporting EMI students

One of the main challenges facing the provision of effective support to students in Japanese EMI programmes is the perception that what students need is limited to language support. The clearest evidence that language support alone is not sufficient could be the fact that writing centres and academic support centres exist in Anglophone contexts and are not only used by ESL students. In the support centre discussed in chapter three, 54 international students who were either bilingual or monolingual speakers of English received support over the year of data collection. Regardless of the medium of instruction, there are some students who require support to succeed and there are usually even more students who will be more successful if they receive support. A belief that students only need language support could lead to crucial support needs not being met. Perhaps even more problematic is that this belief could lead to the exclusion of certain groups of students, such as native speakers of English or returnees, from the support offerings. In response to the question "What kinds of systematic support are offered at your university?", one participant responded that:

> One possible reason that no support system has been created is that the English ability of the students in this program is very high—native or close to native. Furthermore, the program is rather small, with only about 30 freshmen entering each year. When the program was originally being planned, it was expected that some students would need English-language support. However, because admissions policies ended up excluding students who had come through the Japanese educational system and imposing high English-ability requirements for applicants from non-English-speaking countries, that support has turned out not to be necessary.

Another challenge facing EMI programme administrators in Japan is the way in which students are classified. This problem is not limited to Japan; many universities around the world have similar issues, which pose difficulties in identifying students who may benefit from language support. In Japan, any student who is a Japanese citizen is classified as a domestic student (and often referred to as a Japanese student), while those who are not citizens are classified as international students. There are administrative purposes for which students need to be classified and the classification used in Japan is probably as good as any other option. The challenge is brought about not by the classification itself, but by assumptions that are made about students falling into each group. If someone is a Japanese student, it is often assumed that they have lived in Japan for a long time and that Japanese is their first language. There are Japanese citizens who have lived for a long time outside of Japan and who either have another first language or are bilingual in Japanese and another language. Similarly, there are Japanese non-citizens who are classified as international students but who have lived all or most of their life in Japan, for whom Japanese may be their first language or they may be bilingual in Japanese and another language. Offering support specifically for Japanese students or for international students, is an oversimplification of students' real situations and real needs. It would seem preferable to offer a range of support options and allow students to choose the kinds of support they use.

Even when administrators provide flexible options, allowing any students to receive any kind of support, in some cases, students have assumptions about the needs of other students based on such classifications. The support centre discussed in chapter three employed any kind of students at the university, regardless of ethnicity, nationality or student status. I repeatedly encountered traditional Japanese background students who had completed their schooling in Japan and did not have extensive experience abroad feeling anxiety about offering tutorial sessions to international students from Anglophone contexts or returnee students. In most cases, such students asked me whether I could ask another tutor to take over the sessions. In all cases, they made this request before having met the student or having tried to support them. Thus, I frequently had to reassure students that they were capable of providing support to any student at the university and persuade them to have at least one session with the tutee they had been assigned before determining whether or not they were an appropriate tutor to provide support. There was not a single case in which the tutor came back to me after one session and asked me to assign another tutor. There were a large number of cases in which tutors from traditional Japanese educational backgrounds provided support to native English speaking tutees that the tutees found useful. Holding assumptions about other people based on their ethnicity, nationality or student status can cause anxiety and a lack of confidence in oneself. Similarly, centres that reinforce such assumptions by employing international students over Japanese students in peer support roles may reinforce such a lack of confidence in Japanese students who would be capable of effectively supporting their peers but are not provided with the opportunity to build their confidence in this way.

Typically, educational institutions hope to provide as many opportunities for learning as possible to all the students they admit. The research discussed in this book demonstrates that important learning takes place for both tutors and tutees in peer support tutorial sessions. Yet these learning opportunities are not available to students in universities where no support is offered. The learning opportunities involved in tutoring other students, which have been found in previous research to be greater than those involved in receiving tutorial support (Astin, 1993; Lansiquot & Rosalia, 2015; Pascarella & Terenzini, 2005), are not available to students in universities where only instructors or professional support staff are employed in support roles. Furthermore, these opportunities are not available to Japanese students in universities where only international students are employed in peer support roles. Making efforts to increase the amount of support offered to students, along with the range of support offerings, to increase the use of peers as providers of support and to increase the use of Japanese domestic students as providers of support are all likely to be significant in increasing opportunities for learning in EMI programmes in Japan.

References

Astin, A. (1993). *What matters in college: Four critical years revisited.* Jossey-Bass.

Lansiquot, R. & Rosalia, C. (2015). Online peer review: Encouraging student response and development. *Journal of Interactive Learning Research, 26*(1), 105–123.

McKinley, J. (2010). English language writing centres in Japanese universities: What do students really need? *Studies in Self-Access Learning Journal, 1*(1), 17–31.

Pascarella, E. & Terenzini, P. (2005). *How college affects students: A third decade of research.* Jossey-Bass.

Appendix A
Survey on student support for English-medium instruction

1. Your university was selected to participate in this research on the basis of having at least one EMI degree program and/or department. For the purpose of this research, an EMI program/department is defined as a department in which all the classes that a student needs to graduate are offered in English. Please confirm that this was the case at your university in the 2016 academic year.

   a. Yes, there is at least one program/department in which all the classes that a student needs to graduate are offered in English.
   b. No, there are no programs/departments in which all the classes that a student needs to graduate are offered in English.

2. For how long has your university been offering EMI programs?

   a. 10 years or more
   b. 7–9 years
   c. 4–6 years
   d. Only the last 1–3 years

3. What is the dominant purpose of EMI instruction at your university?

   a. Language education
   b. Both language education and subject learning
   c. Subject learning

4. This research is investigating the support offered to students to help them succeed in their EMI studies. Please answer this question to help us understand the students in the EMI program at your university. To the best of your knowledge, what percentage of the students in the EMI degree program or department at your university are Japanese domestic students?

a. None
b. 1–20%
c. 21–40%
d. 41–60%
e. 61–80%
f. 81–99%
g. All

5. Is there any systematic/organized support offered outside of the classroom to students who are studying in the English medium? (Excluding any help offered outside of the classroom by the classroom teacher)

    a. Yes
    b. No

6. What kinds of support are offered at your university? Please select all that apply.

    a. A self-access center
    b. Listening skills support
    c. Reading skills support
    d. Speaking skills support
    e. Writing skills support
    f. Other (please specify)

7. In which language(s) is the support offered?

    a. English only
    b. Both Japanese and English
    c. Japanese only

8. Who can receive the support? (Please choose all that apply)

    a. Japanese domestic students
    b. Returnees
    c. Short-term international exchange students
    d. International degree-seeking students

9. Who provides the support?

    a. Instructors at the university
    b. Dedicated learning support staff
    c. International undergraduate students
    d. Japanese undergraduate students
    e. International postgraduate students
    f. Japanese postgraduate students

10. In your own words, please describe the kind(s) of systematic/organized support offered outside of the classroom at your university. Please provide as much detail as possible.

11. How often can students receive the support?

    a. Up to once a week
    b. 2–4 times a week
    c. 5–7 times a week
    d. More than 7 times a week
    e. Other (please specify)

12. How long can a student receive support during each support session?

    a. Up to 30 minutes
    b. 31–60 minutes
    c. 61–90 minutes
    d. 91–120 minutes
    e. More than 120 minutes
    f. Other (please specify)

13. At what stage(s) in their studies can students receive support?

    a. In the 1st year only
    b. In the first 2 years
    c. In the first 3 years
    d. All 4 years
    e. Other (please specify)

14. Is the support optional or compulsory?

    a. Completely optional
    b. Compulsory for a limited time
    c. Compulsory for some students
    d. Compulsory for all students

Appendix B
Tutors' feedback questionnaire

1. During this session, did you learn anything about this tutee?

    Yes (Please write the details in the box below)   No

2. During this session, did you learn anything about tutoring?

    Yes (Please write details in the box below)   No

3. During this session, did you learn anything about the subject you were tutoring?

    Yes (Please write details in the box below)   No

4. How well do you think the session went?
    a. Very well
    b. Somewhat well
    c. Not so well
    d. Terrible

    Please explain what went well and/or not so well in this session (Optional)

Appendix C
Tutees' feedback questionnaire

1. Do you think your tutor understood your needs?

    Yes   No

2. During this session, did you learn anything new?

    Yes (Please write details in the box below)   No

    ┌─────────────────────────────────────┐
    │   │
    │   │
    │   │
    └─────────────────────────────────────┘

3. How confident do you currently feel in the subject?
    a. I am capable of doing very well
    b. I am capable of doing somewhat well
    c. I am not capable of doing very well
    d. I am completely incapable

4. How well do you think the session went?
    a. Very well
    b. Somewhat well
    c. Not so well
    d. Terribly

    ┌───┐
    │ Please explain what went well and/or not so well in this session (Optional) │
    │   │
    │   │
    │   │
    │   │
    └───┘

Index

academic challenge 26, 113–114
academic skills support 48–49, 51, 66, 68–70, 114–116
academic support centre 47–49, 60–88, 111
Ammon, U. 6, 14
Astin, A. 84, 119

Bradford, A. 13, 14, 15, 16, 17, 20, 27, 29, 49
Brown, H. 5, 7, 8, 10, 11, 12, 16, 33

challenges: for faculty 13–17; for students 9–13
Coleman, J. 6, 15, 16

definitions of EMI 1, 30–32
domestic students 3–4, 5, 6–7, 18, 26, 28, 34, 36–38, 39, 42, 48–49, 110, 113, 117–118

English for Academic Purposes (EAP) 2, 10–11, 115
evaluation of support 47–49, 56–58, 106–107

Galloway, N. 12, 14, 17

instructors in support roles 37–38, 96–97, 118–119
intercultural competence 3–4, 5, 17, 18, 116
international student advisors 29
international students 3, 5, 6, 8, 15, 16, 17, 18, 19, 26, 28, 29, 36–38, 39, 42, 48–49, 51, 56, 59, 110, 113, 117–118
Ishikura, Y. 12, 29, 30

Kelo, M. 12, 14, 17, 18, 24, 26, 27, 28, 42, 50, 51
Kuh, G. 25, 26

language of support 36, 38, 42, 43, 63, 99–100
language proficiency 2, 6–7, 10–13, 14, 19, 27, 37, 42–43, 49–50, 51, 95–96, 114–115
language support 39, 66, 74–75, 114–116, 117
Lassegard, J. 5, 14, 16, 17, 24, 26, 29
learner autonomy 25
learning advising 39
Leask, B. 4, 17, 18, 24, 26–27, 44, 50, 52
listening support 35

Macauley, W. J 47, 57
marketing *see* promotion
mathematics and science support 66, 72–73
McKinley, J. 50, 59, 111–112
mentoring 105, 111
MEXT 3, 4, 7, 8, 30, 31
Morita, L. 7, 30
Murphey, T. 60, 86, 87

native-speakerism 48
need for support 28, 49–52, 91–92

OECD 6, 28, 30, 43

PASS 44, 50
peer support 37–38, 39, 44, 48–49, 51, 53–56, 58, 59, 60–61, 63–64, 66, 97–98, 107–108, 111, 112–113, 116, 118–119
plagiarism 98–99
professional support staff 37–38, 39, 42–43, 58, 96, 112–113, 116, 118–119
promotion 61–62, 104–105, 111

reading support 34–36, 44, 110–111
recruitment 60–61, 100–102, 111
returnees 37, 117–118
Ruegg, R. 14, 87

satisfaction with support 48–49, 57, 64, 66–68, 76–77, 82–83, 112
self-access centres 35, 39

speaking support 35
supervision *see* mentoring

Taguchi, N. 4, 6
test support 36, 66, 70–72
Thompson, G. 48, 50, 59
Topping, K. 56, 84
training 60–61, 102–104, 111
Tsuneyoshi, R. 4, 7, 14, 15, 19, 24, 28, 30

uptake of support 28, 52–53, 111–112
usage of support 47, 49, 50, 64, 66, 81–82, 111–112

Wilkinson, R. 2, 5, 12, 14
writing centres 39, 41, 49–50, 51, 59
writing support 35, 110–111